W9-BNH-992

Lucia stupid

MODERN ENGLISH

second edition

MODERN ENGLISH

exercises for non-native speakers

PART II:
sentences and complex structures

MARCELLA FRANK
New York University

Prentice Hall, Inc.   *Englewood Cliffs, New Jersey 07632*

Editorial/production supervision and
    interior design by Anthony Keating and Eva Jaunzems
Cover design by Ben Santora
Manufacturing buyer: Harry P. Baisley

0-13-593856-2 01

Prentice-Hall International (UK) Limited, *London*
Prentice-Hall of Australia Pty. Limited, *Sydney*
Prentice-Hall of Canada Inc., *Toronto*
Prentice-Hall Hispanoamericana, S.A., *Mexico*
Prentice-Hall of India Private Limited, *New Delhi*
Prentice-Hall of Japan, Inc., *Tokyo*
Prentice-Hall of Southeast Asia Pte. Ltd., *Singapore*
Editora Prentice-Hall do Brasil, Ltda., *Rio de Janeiro*
Whitehall Books Limited, *Wellington, New Zealand*

CONTENTS

Preface to the Second Edition   xi

Preface to the First Edition   xiii

1

SENTENCES   1

1-1 Requests and Commands (Imperative Mood)   2

1-2 Exclamatory Sentences   4

1-3 Joining Sentences Coordinately (Compound
Sentences)   6

1-4 Joining Sentences with Conjunctive Adverbs   7

1-5 Abridgments in Clauses of Short Agreement   11

1-6 Parallel Construction   13

1-7 "Dangling" Constructions   16

2

ADVERBIAL CLAUSES   19

2-1 Types of Adverbial Clauses   21

2-2 Adverbial Clauses of Purpose   24

2-3 Verbs in Time Clauses—Future Time   25

2-4 Verbs in Time Clauses—Past Time   27

2-5 Conditional Clauses with *Unless*   28

2-6 Real Conditions (1) Future Time   29

2-7 Real Conditions (2) General Time   30

2-8 Unreal Conditions (Contrary to Fact)   31

2-9 Real and Unreal Conditional Clauses   33

2-10 Conditional Clauses Beginning with *Were, Had, Should*   34

2-11 Mixed Time in Unreal Conditions   35

2-12 Unreal Conditions in Sentences with *But, Or, Otherwise*   36

2-13 Adverbial Clauses of Result with *So, Such, Such a*   39

2-14 Phrasal Conjunctions in Adverbial Clauses   40

2-15 Review of Adverbial Clauses   41

3

ADJECTIVE CLAUSES

ADJECTIVE CLAUSES **45**

3-1 Punctuation of Adjective Clauses   46

3-2 Case of Relative Pronouns Introducing Adjective Clauses   47

3-3 Relative Pronouns as Objects of Prepositions   49

3-4 Relative Pronouns Patterning Like *Some of Which* and *Some of Whom*   51

3-5 Adjective Clauses used in Definition   52

3-6 Review of Adjective Clauses   53

4

NOUN CLAUSES

NOUN CLAUSES **57**

4-1 Sequence of Tenses in Noun Clauses (1)   58

4-2 Sequence of Tenses in Noun Clauses (2)   61

4-3 Noun Clauses Objects from Statements, Questions, Exclamations   62

4-4 Noun Clauses after Wish (1) Referring to Present Time   63

4-5 Noun Clauses after Wish (2) Referring to Past Time   65

4-6 Noun Clauses after Wish vs Unreal Conditional Clauses   66

4-7 Noun Clauses with Infinitive Abridgment 70

4-8 *That* Clauses after Verbs of Urgency 72

4-9 *That* Clauses after Adjectives of Urgency 74

4-10 Review of Noun Clauses 75

5

PARTICIPIAL PHRASES 79

5-1 Forms of Participles (1) 80

5-2 Forms of Participles (2) 82

5-3 Punctuation and Position of Participial Phrases 84

5-4 Participial Phrases in Two-Part Objects of Verbs 86

5-5 Participial Phrases to Express Means or Manner 87

5-6 Participial Phrases as Alternatives for Adverbial Clauses 89

5-7 Instructions with *Have* + Past Participle 91

5-8 Review of Participial Phrases 94

6

GERUND PHRASES 97

6-1 Forms of Gerunds 97

6-2 "Subjects" in Gerund Phrases 99

6-3 *The* + Gerund + *Of* Phrase "Object" 103

6-4 Gerund Phrase Objects of Verbs 104

6-5 Gerund Phrase Objects of Prepositions 106

6-6 Adjectives-from-Adverbs in Gerund Phrases 108

6-7 Review of Gerund Phrases 110

7

INFINITIVE PHRASES 113

7-1 Forms of Infinitives 113

7-2 *For* "Subjects" of Infinitive Phrases 115

7-3 Anticipatory *It* with Infinitive Phrase Subjects 116

7-4 *Of, To* "Subjects" of Infinitive Phrases   118

7-5 Infinitive Phrases as Objects of Verbs   122

7-6 Infinitive vs. Gerund Subjects   125

7-7 Infinitive vs. Gerund Objects   127

7-8 *To*-Less Infinitives or *-ing* Participles in Two-Part
Objects   129

7-9 Infinitive Phrases as Alternatives for Adjective
Clauses   132

7-10 Infinitive Phrases as Alternatives for Adverbial
Clauses   133

7-11 Infinitives Plus Prepositional Particles   135

7-12 Infinitive Phrases after *Too, Enough*   137

7-13 Review of Infinitive Phrases   138

8

ABSOLUTE CONSTRUCTIONS 141

8-1 Absolute Constructions with Participles   142

8-2 Absolute Constructions without Participles   145

8-3 *With* Absolute Constructions   146

8-4 Position of Absolute Constructions   148

8-5 Review of Absolute Constructions   150

9

ABSTRACT NOUN PHRASES 153

9-1 Form of Abstract Nouns   153

9-2 "Subjects" in Abstract Noun Phrases   154

9-3 "Objects" in Abstract Noun Phrases (1)   156

9-4 "Objects" in Abstract Noun Phrases (2)   158

9-5 "Complements" of Nouns in Abstract Noun
Phrases   159

9-6 Adjectives-from-Adverbs in Abstract Noun
Phrases   161

9-7 Abstract Noun Phrases as Alternatives for
Dependent Clauses   162

9-8 Review of Abstract Noun Phrases   164

10

APPOSITIVE PHRASES 167

10-1 Changing Adjective Clauses to Appositive Phrases   167

10-2 "Complements" of Appositive Nouns and Adjectives   169

10-3 Position of Appositive Phrases   172

10-4 Review of Appositive Phrases   174

FINAL REVIEW 177

Coordinate and Subordinate Sentence Structures   177

Adverbials   180

Adjectivals   185

Nominals (Noun Structures)   188

APPENDIX 1: PRACTICE TESTS 195

Structure Test 1   195

Structure Test 2   197

APPENDIX 2: PRACTICE FOR THE TOEFL TEST 203

1 Correcting Sentence Faults   204

2 Improving Sentences (1)   207

3 Improving Sentences (2)   210

4 Subject-Verb Agreement   212

5 Verbs—Auxiliaries (1)   215

6 Verbs—Tenses (2)   218

7 Verbals   222

8 Word Order (1)   223

9 Word Order (2)   225

10 Word Forms   228

11 Prepositions (1)   231

12 Prepositions (2)   232

13 Pronouns   235

14 Comparison   239

15 Articles—General Rules (1)   242

16 Articles—*The* in Names (2)   245

ANSWERS TO TOEFL PREPARATION SECTION FOR PART II **249**

1 Correcting Sentence Faults   249

2 Improving Sentences (1)   250

3 Improving Sentences (2)   251

4 Subject-Verb Agreement   252

5 Verbs—Auxiliaries (1)   252

6 Verbs—Tenses (2)   252

7 Verbals   252

8 Word Order (1)   253

9 Word Order (2)   253

10 Word Forms   254

11 Prepositions (1)   254

12 Prepositions (2)   254

13 Pronouns   255

14 Comparison   255

15 Articles—General Rules (1)   255

16 Articles—The in Names (2)   255

Preface
to the Second Edition

This new edition of *Modern English: Exercises for Non-native Speakers* retains the format of the first edition. The teacher will find the same carefully presented exercises that offer a wide range of practice in a systematic manner. Most of the exercises from the first edition have been kept, but some have been shortened to make room for others that are equally useful. I have replaced or revised sentences that were not clearcut examples of the usage being studied or that teachers found objectionable or outdated. Also, I have tried to clarify some of the explanations and instructions. Finally, I have omitted the summarizing exercises at the end of each chapter in Part Two.

This second edition has several new features that should increase its usefulness.

1. Reviews have been added to the texts:

   To Part One, a review for each chapter. Review sentences have been taken mainly from the sentences already in the chapter. These reviews can also be used as tests.

   To Part Two, a final review section of all the structures in Part Two. Each exercise in this section gives practice in combining sentences to produce several possible structures rather than just one structure. Students have the chance here to see which grammatical structures are available for the same meaning. Integrated within this practice are the punctuation, position, variety of usage, or possible omission of some structure words.

2. Objective tests have been added to both Part I and Part II. The test items in Part One cover mainly the structures practiced in this part. In Part Two, the test items include structures studied in both volumes.

3. In Part Two, a brief section has been added to give students help in preparing for the TOEFL test. This section covers problems in agreement and number, fragments and run-on sentences, verb tenses, verbals, word forms, word order, prepositions and conjunctions, articles, comparison, parallelism, repetition.

4. The instructor's manual that accompanies this second edition has been expanded to give not only the complete answers to the exercises but also abundant guidance to teachers using the books. There are further explanations of some of the structures, and suggestions on how to introduce the practice on many of the structures, as well as how to use some of them in communicative situations.

5. The answers have been set up in the manual in such a way that they can be reproduced for use by students for self-study.

Students who use these workbooks have available to them two of my reference books. Advanced students can get reference information from *Modern English: A Practical Reference Guide* (Prentice-Hall, Englewood Cliffs, N.J., 1972). Less advanced students can refer to my recently published *Writer's Companion* (Prentice-Hall, Englewood Cliffs, N.J., 1983), a small, compact guide to usage and writing.

At this time, I wish to express my appreciation to Robin Baliszewski, Brenda White, and Eva Jaunzems of Prentice-Hall, Inc. for their great help in seeing this second edition through to completion.

Marcella Frank
New York, New York

Preface
to the First Edition

The purpose of the two volumes of *Modern English: Exercises for Non-native Speakers* is to provide advanced students of English as a foreign language with much carefully controlled and integrated practice on points of usage that continue to trouble such students. While the emphasis of these exercises is on written work, many of them may be used for oral drill as well.

The exercises are arranged systematically for ease of location. They progress from the less difficult to the more difficult, from strict control to looser control. Explanations are kept to a minimum; students understand what they are to do from the examples, many of which are given in contrast.

It would be desirable to use the workbooks in conjunction with *Modern English: A Practical Reference Guide* (Prentice-Hall, Englewood Cliffs, N.J., 1972), which describes in detail the facts of usage on which the practice in the workbooks is based. However, the exercises have been set up so that the workbooks can be used independently of the reference guide.

The chapters in the workbooks are correlated with the chapters in the reference book. Thus, the sequence of practice moves from usage connected with the parts of speech to usage connected with the complex syntactic structures. As in the reference guide, the chapters on parts of speech have been influenced by structural grammar, those on complex syntactic structures by transformational grammar.

PART I:
PARTS OF SPEECH

Each chapter on a part of speech begins with a chart outlining the structural features of the part of speech (function, position, form, markers). This outline is based on the description in *Modern English: A Practical Reference Guide*. Then come many exercises on word forms (inflectional and derivational suffixes, spelling peculiarities and irregularities), word order and other troublesome usages connected with each part of speech.

PART II:
SENTENCES AND COMPLEX STRUCTURES

The complex structures that have been chosen for practice are those derived from simple basic sentences. Mastery of these structures is especially important for writing since they provide grammatical shapes for the expression of predications and thus relate grammar to meaning. The structures that are included are clauses, verbals, abstract noun phrases, and appositive phrases.

Each chapter on the complex structures is introduced by a chart that illustrates the various types of the structure. This is followed by transformational exercises involving: a) changes from the basic subject-verb-complement; b) the position(s) of the structure; c) the punctuation of the structure; d) substitutions for the structure; e) abridgment of the structure. At the end of each chapter is an exercise requiring a one-sentence summary of a paragraph.

I wish to acknowledge my special indebtedness to Milton G. Saltzer, Associate Director of the American Language Institute, New York University, for making it possible for me to try out a preliminary edition of these workbooks for several semesters at our Institute. Thanks are also due to my colleagues for their useful suggestions and comments, and to the students of the American Language Institute for helping me see which exercises needed improvement or change.

M.F.

1

Sentences

TYPES OF SENTENCES

1. *Simple sentence*—Contains one full subject and predicate. Takes the form of:
   a. *a statement*
   b. *a question*
   c. *a request or command*

   d. *an exclamation*

He lives in New York.

How old are you?

Please close the door. (The subject *you* is understood.)

What a terrible temper she has!

2. *Compound sentence*—Contains two or more sentences joined into one by:
   a. *punctuation alone*

   b. *punctuation and a conjunctive adverb*

   c. *a coordinate conjunction (and, or, but, yet, so, for)*
   When such sentences are joined coordinately, they are each called independent clauses.

The weather was very bad; all classes were canceled.

The weather was very bad; therefore all classes were canceled.

The weather was very bad, so all classes were canceled.

3. *Complex sentence*—Contains one or more dependent (or subordinate) clauses. A dependent clause contains a full subject and predicate beginning with a word that attaches the clause to an independent clause (called the main clause).
   a. *adverbial clause*

   b. *adjective clause*

   c. *noun clause*

All classes were canceled because the weather was bad.

Children who are under twelve years must be accompanied by their parents.

I can't understand why you did such a thing.

4. *Compound-complex sentence*—Contains two or more independent clauses and one or more dependent clauses. | All classes were canceled because the weather was bad, and students were told to listen to the radio to find out when classes would begin again.

COORDINATION WITHIN SENTENCES—WITH *AND, OR, BUT*

Words	He works **quickly** and **efficiently**.
Phrases	**Bored by the conversation,** but **not wanting to leave,** he walked out into the garden.
Clauses	He said **that he was tired** and **that he was going to bed**.

SUBORDINATION WITHIN SENTENCES—NOMINAL, ADJECTIVAL, OR ADVERBIAL ELEMENTS

	Nominal (Noun) Function	Adjectival Function	Adverbial Function
Words	**Sports** are enjoyable.	She bought an **expensive** lamp.	He came **unwillingly**.
Phrases	*gerund*—**Swimming in the lake** is fun. *infinitive*—**To swim in the lake** is fun.	*prepositional*—The lamp **on the table** is expensive. *participial*—The lamp **standing on the table** is expensive.	*prepositional*—He came **against his will**.
Clauses	**That he should enjoy sports** is understandable.	The lamp **which is standing on the table** is expensive.	He came **although he was unwilling**.

All complex structures are either clauses or phrases, and function as nouns, adjectives or adverbs. Clauses contain *full subjects and predicates*. Phrases are of two kinds. A phrase that begins with a preposition is called a *prepositional phrase;* a phrase that begins with a form from a verb (either a participle or an infinitive) is called a *verbal phrase*.

1-1
REQUESTS AND COMMANDS
(IMPERATIVE MOOD)

The simple form of the verb is used for requests, commands, or instructions.

Second person, singular and plural:

Open the door.
Don't open the door.

First and second person together:

Let's open the door.
Let's not open the door.
(Here the request takes the form of a suggestion.)

An adverb may precede the imperative verb:

Always open that door slowly.
Don't **ever** open that door.

Formulas of politeness such as **please, will** (or **would**) **you please** often accompany requests.

Change the following sentences to imperative form.

EXAMPLE: a. You must cook the meat very slowly.
<u>Cook the meat very slowly.</u>

b. You shouldn't do your homework when you're tired.
<u>Don't do your homework when you're tired.</u>

c. We should take a break soon.
<u>Let's take a break soon.</u>

1. You must never leave this door unlocked.

_____

2. You will first go to the post office and then to the bank.

_____

3. We must not encourage him to believe we can help him.

_____

4. You must always obey your father even when he seems too strict.

_____

5. To get the right color, you must mix equal parts of red and blue.

_____

6. We shouldn't waste so much time with small details.

_____

7. To get there, you must turn right at the bridge.

_____

8. You shouldn't ever listen to him.

_____

9. You will deliver this package at once.

_____

10. You and I should take care of this right away. We shouldn't wait any longer.

_____

_____

11. We should hurry if we want to get home in time for dinner.

_____

12. As soon as you hear from them, you must let us know.

_____

13. When you leave the house, you must turn off all the lights and you must close all the windows.

_____

_____

1-2
EXCLAMATORY SENTENCES

Exclamations may begin with **what** or **how.**

What—a noun ends the exclamatory phrase

> **What delicious fruit** this is!¹
> **What delicious pineapples** these are!
> **What a delicious pineapple** this is!

How—an adjective or adverb ends the exclamatory phrase

> **How graceful** she is!
> **How gracefully** she dances!

The subject and the verb in an exclamatory sentence retain normal word order except in poetic or literary style—**How green was my valley!**

Change the following statements to exclamations. Begin with **what, what a,** or **how.** Be sure to put the subject before the verb.

EXAMPLE: a. She has a pleasant personality.
   What a pleasant personality she has!

   b. These are expensive towels.
   What expensive towels these are!

   c. This lecture is boring.
   How boring this lecture is!

   d. He walks awkwardly.
   How awkwardly he walks!

¹An exclamatory sentence may also end with a period—**What delicious food this is.**
The period lessens the impact of the exclamation.

1. He has just made a stupid remark.

_____

2. The store was crowded yesterday.

_____

3. The fire was put out quickly.

_____

4. She wears old-fashioned clothes.

_____

5. The children are behaving well today.

_____

6. He has told an amusing story.

_____

7. The plane is going fast.

_____

8. A terrible mistake has been made.

_____

9. He is an extraordinary man.

_____

10. This author has written many books.[2]

_____

11. He has spent much money for those flowers.[2]

_____

12. He has behaved badly toward you.

_____

13. This lesson is difficult.

_____

14. Much work was done for nothing.[2]

_____

15. He is riding in an old car.[3]

_____

16. She lives in a large city.[3]

_____

[2]Use **how** with **much, many.**
[3]A preposition that is part of the exclamatory phrase usually appears in final position—**What terrible trouble he is _in_!**

1-3

JOINING SENTENCES COORDINATELY
(COMPOUND SENTENCES)

Sentences may be joined by punctuation alone, by coordinate conjunctions, or by conjunctive adverbs. The two parts of such combined sentences are coordinate clauses; that is, the clauses are grammatically equal.

1. Joined by punctuation alone—**John was sick; he didn't come to school.**
2. Joined by a coordinate conjunction[4]—**John was sick, so he didn't come to school.**
3. Joined by a conjunctive adverb—**John was sick; therefore, he didn't come to school.**

Note that a *semicolon* replaces the period of the first sentence except when a coordinate conjunction joins the clauses. If both clauses are short, the comma may be omitted before a coordinate conjunction. If one or both clauses are long, the part with the conjunctive adverb, or even with the coordinate conjunction, may be separated to form a new sentence.

Combine each group of sentences in the three ways just given—by punctuation alone, by coordinate conjunctions, and by conjunctive adverbs.

EXAMPLE: John was sick. He came to school anyhow.

John was sick; he came to school anyhow.

John was sick, but he came to school. (*Anyhow* is replaced by *but.*)

John was sick; however, he came to school. (*Anyhow* is repaced by *however.*)

1. Mr. Smith was very angry at his boss's order.
   He decided to obey it anyhow.

_____

_____

_____

2. Mr. Smith was very angry at his boss's order.
   He decided to disobey it.

_____

_____

_____

3. Mr. Smith doesn't like his aunt.
   He invited her to his wedding anyhow.

_____

_____

_____

[4]The coordinate conjunctions are *and, but, or, nor, for, yet.*

4. Mr. Smith doesn't like his aunt.
   He won't invite her to his wedding.

   _____

   _____

   _____

5. The young man needs a car for his work.
   He is going to buy one right away.

   _____

   _____

   _____

6. The young man doesn't need a car for his work.
   He is going to buy one anyhow.

   _____

   _____

   _____

7. The new student was very shy.
   The teacher didn't call on him.

   _____

   _____

   _____

8. The new student was very shy.
   The teacher called on him several times anyhow.

   _____

   _____

   _____

1-4
JOINING SENTENCES WITH CONJUNCTIVE ADVERBS

Most conjunctive adverbs are found in formal writing rather than in informal conversation. Some of the more common conjunctive adverbs are listed below.

Addition	moreover, in addition, besides, furthermore
Condition	otherwise
Concession	however, still, nevertheless
Result	therefore, consequently, thus

beside

Besides, still are less formal than the other conjunctive adverbs; **nevertheless, consequently** are more formal.

The position of conjunctive adverbs is like that of other adverbs. They may appear:

At the beginning	He doesn't like his job; **however,** he won't leave until he finds another job.
With the verb	He doesn't like his job; he won't leave, **however,** until he finds another job.
At the end	He doesn't like his job; he won't leave until he finds another job, **however.**
	(Note that this final position is less desirable because the relationship intended by **however** is suspended too long.)

The punctuation of conjunctive adverbs is also like that of other adverbs. The writer uses commas to reflect a pause in speech.

A. Combine each group of sentences with one of the conjunctive adverbs. *Use a semicolon to replace the period of the first sentence;* use a comma to cut off the conjunctive adverb if the comma reflects a pause in speech for you. Note which of the three adverbial positions seems most desirable for the conjunctive adverb.

EXAMPLE: a.   Mr. Smith is an intelligent and stimulating teacher.
Also, he is interested in his students. (omit *also*)

Mr. Smith is an intelligent and stimulating teacher; moreover (*or* in addition), he is interested in his students.

b.   We must all eat the proper food.
If we don't, we'll get sick. (omit *if we don't*)

We must all eat the proper food; otherwise (,)^5 we'll get sick.   *or* ....; we'll get sick otherwise. (an acceptable choice because the second clause is short)

c.   There are many people who like to buy on the installment plan.
I prefer to buy for cash.

There are many people who like to buy on the installment plan; however, I prefer to buy for cash.

or ...; I prefer, however,   *or* ...; I, however, prefer   *or* ...; I prefer to buy for cash, however.

d.   There is no demand in the United States for the type of car you sell.
I cannot give you an order for this car.

There is no demand in the United States for the type of car you sell; therefore, I cannot give you an order for this car.   *or* ...; I therefore cannot   *or* I cannot (,) therefore (,)

1.   John is a very lazy student.
Also, he always comes late to class. (omit *also*)

_____

_____

^{5}In a grammar text, parentheses around a comma indicate that the comma can be omitted. A comma is more common with words like *however* and less common with *otherwise*.

2. She didn't study hard enough.
    If she had, she would have passed the examination. (omit *if she had*)

    _____

    _____

3. He seems to be a very intelligent and able man.
    I don't think he is suited for this particular job.

    _____

    _____

4. There is very little rain in this region.
    We often have crop failures.

    _____

    _____

5. Keep off my property.
    If you don't, I'll have you arrested. (omit *if you don't*)

    _____

    _____

6. Jim's mother doesn't like animals in the house.
    She has refused to let him get a dog.

    _____

    _____

7. It's too late to go to the movies.
    Also, I don't like the picture they're playing. (omit *also*)

    _____

    _____

8. Recreation is good for everyone.
    As in all things, we must not go to extremes.

    _____

    _____

9. The weather has been extremely cold all winter long.
    They are going to Miami Beach to get some sunshine.

    _____

    _____

10. Their car is very old.
    It has never given them any trouble.

    _____

    _____

11.   You should get the license right away.
       If you don't, you'll have to pay a fine. (omit *if you don't*)

_____

_____

12.   The philanthropist made a large contribution for the university library.
       Also, he gave some money for a scholarship fund for needy students. (omit *also*)

_____

_____

13.   You must do as the doctor says.
       If you don't, you may get sick again. (omit *if you don't*)

_____

_____

14.   He's studying harder now.
       His grades in school are still poor.

_____

_____

B. Coordinate conjunctions provide the most informal means of connecting sentences. Unlike conjunctive adverbs, coordinate conjunctions can only be placed *before* the second part of the sentence.
   Join the groups of sentences in A by the coordinate conjunctions *and, or, but, so,* or *for.*

EXAMPLE: a. **and** (addition)
             Mr. Smith is an intelligent and stimulating teacher, *and* he is interested in his students.

             b. **or** (condition)
             We must all eat the proper food, *or* we'll get sick.

             c. **but** (concession)
             There are many people who like to buy on the installment plan, *but* I prefer to buy for cash.

             d. **so** (result)
             There is no demand in the United States for the type of car you sell, *so* I cannot give you an order for this car.

             or

             for (cause)
             I cannot give you an order for this car, *for* there is no demand. . . .
             (The use of *for* to express cause is restricted mainly to formal usage.)

ABRIDGMENTS IN CLAUSES OF SHORT AGREEMENT

Clauses may be shortened by substituting an auxiliary for an entire predicate. Such abridgment is especially common in clauses of short agreement or disagreement.

John likes the movies	{ *or*	, and **his wife does too.**
		, and **so does his wife.**
John doesn't like the movies	{ *or*	, and **his wife doesn't either.**
		, and **neither does his wife.**
John likes the movies		, but **his wife doesn't.**
John doesn't like the movies		, but **his wife does.**

Note the reversal of subject and auxiliary after **so, neither.**

A. Use the words in parentheses to make a short statement of agreement. Give the forms of agreement with too or either.

EXAMPLE: a. The walls are painted white. (the ceiling)
The walls are painted white, and the ceiling is too.

b. The geometry books haven't arrived. (the algebra books)
The geometry books haven't arrived, and the algebra books haven't, either.

1. Your sister called today. (your brother)

_____

2. Mary finished her homework early. (Jane)

_____

3. The rugs haven't been cleaned yet. (the drapes)

_____

4. My country wants peace. (all the other countries)

_____

5. A hawk can fly. (a dove)

_____

6. Their car won't start in this cold. (ours)

_____

7. The students enjoyed the play. (their teacher)

_____

8. Jean dances very gracefully. (her sisters)

_____

9. I've never read that book. (my friend)

_____

10. The younger students have already been fed. (the older students)

_____

11. That apple isn't ripe. (this apple)

_____

12. My friend failed the examination. (I)

_____

13. We don't need any help. (she)

_____

14 A woman was hurt in the accident. (Her two daughters)

_____

B. Use the sentences in A to make the alternate forms of agreement with **so** or **neither**. Keep in mind that *the subject and the auxiliary must be reversed.*

EXAMPLE: a. The walls are painted white. (the ceiling)
The walls are painted white and so is the ceiling.

b. The geometry books haven't arrived. (the algebra books)
The geometry books haven't arrived and neither have the algebra books.

C. Supply the appropriate auxiliary, then restate the sentence by reversing the positive-negative contrast.

EXAMPLE: a. He goes swimming every day, but his sister <u>doesn't</u>.
He doesn't go swimming every day, but his sister does.

b. The cat doesn't like to be in the snow, but the dog <u>does</u>.
The cat likes to be in the snow, but the dog doesn't.

1. These books belong to me, but those _____.

_____

2. The first bus didn't arrive on time, but the second one _____.

_____

3. Marie will come to the party, but her husband _____.

_____

4. The large picture looks good over the sofa, but the small one _____.

_____

5. This room isn't well lit, but that one _____.

_____

6. The green dress can be washed by hand, but the blue one _____.

_____

7. Her father liked her new boyfriend, but her mother _____.

_____

8. I can ice skate, but my friend _____.

_____

9. Her sister will bring the children, but her brother _____.

_____

10. This pot leaks, but that one _____.

_____

11. She has never been to Europe but her children _____.

_____

12. The salesgirls in this store are helpful, but those in the next store _____.

_____

1-6
PARALLEL CONSTRUCTION

Words, phrases, or clauses joined by the coordinate conjunctions **and, or, but** have *the same grammatical form* (parallelism).

> Her **long illness** and **slow recovery** made her very despondent. (two nouns joined by **and**).
>
> She doesn't like **to get up in the morning** or **to go to bed at night.** (two infinitive phrases joined by **or**)
>
> He told us **that his wife had been in an accident** but **that luckily she had not been hurt.** (two **that** clauses joined by **but**)

Parallel forms are also required with the paired coordinate conjunctions (correlatives)— **both . . . and, (n)either . . . (n)or, not only . . . but also.**

> They are either **at their country home** or **at the beach.**

Elements contrasted with **not** are likewise put in parallel form.

> He always does **what he wants to do**, not **what he should do.**

Informal usage permits the omission of a short structure word like **to, that, at** from the last item—**They are either at their country home or the beach.** In formal usage it is advisable to repeat such a word.

Make the items in parentheses grammatically parallel to the italicized items that precede **and, or, but** or **not.**

EXAMPLE: He spends his spare time *playing golf* and (collect, stamps).
  He spends his spare time playing golf and collecting stamps.

1. Speaking *boldly* and (clear), he explained to the owners why the miners were on strike.

_____

_____

2. I don't know *whether I will get the job* or (I, like, it, after I get it).

_____

_____

3. *Having no money* but (not, want, anyone, to know), he simply said he would go without dinner.

_____

_____

4. He asked *when the apartment would be available* and (how much, it, cost).

_____

_____

5. He did it *because he had to do it,* not (he, wanted to).

_____

_____

6. He was fired not only *because of his inexcusable absences from the office,* but (he, was, inefficient).

_____

_____

7. It is frustrating *to spend so much money* and (achieve, so little).

_____

_____

8. After *seeing the preacher in person* and (hear, him, speak), she began to have more respect for him.

_____

_____

9. He is the kind of person who both *admits his mistake* and (try, to do better, the next time).

_____

_____

Correct the items in parentheses so that they are grammatically parallel to the items that precede **and, or, but** or **not.**

EXAMPLE: I like the painting but not (how it is framed).

I like the painting but not the way it is framed.   *or* . . . but not the frame.

1. He spends his summer weekends either playing tennis or (at the beach).

_____

_____

2. Wanting to accomplish something and (if you actually accomplish it) may not be the same thing.

_____

_____

3. There are two kinds of friends; the casual acquaintance and (the friend who is intimate).

_____

_____

4. There is a great difference between dining out and (to have a snack at home).

_____

_____

5. Slowly and (in a hesitant manner), he addressed the audience before him.

_____

_____

6. He donated a great deal of money, either because he is generous or (because of his desire to get his name into the paper).

_____

_____

7. Here are the rules for winning a tennis match: develop a good serve and (you must keep your eye on the ball).

_____

_____

8. We should judge people by what they do, not by (outward appearances).

_____

_____

1-7
"DANGLING" CONSTRUCTIONS

Many introductory structures that do not contain their own "subjects" within them depend on the subject of the main clause for their agent (the "doer" of the action expressed by the structure).

Preparing breakfast in too much of a hurry, she burned the toast.

After eating dinner, she cleared the table.

To study properly, a person should have good light.

Fearless as a youth, he became more timid as he grew older.

At the age of seven, he came to the United States.

Such introductory elements usually correspond to the predicate parts of simple sentences. If the subjects that follow cannot serve as their agents, the introductory structures are considerd as "dangling," that is, left hanging without a specific word to attach it to.

Dangling

Preparing breakfast in too much of a hurry, the toast was burned.

After eating dinner, the table was cleared.

Certain introductory participial elements have their own "subjects" and therefore do not depend on the subject of the sentence for their agent.

The floods having ruined their crops, many farmers in the area decided to give up their farms.

Make whatever changes are necessary to correct sentences that contain "dangling" introductory elements. (Some sentences are correct.)

EXAMPLE: Believing she had done the right thing, no one could convince her that she was wrong.

Believing she had done the right thing, she could not be convinced that she was wrong.

(The subject, **she**, is the agent of **believing**.)

or Because she believed she had done the right thing, no one could convince her that she was wrong.

(The **because** clause now contains its own subject, **she**.)

1.   While waiting for the doctor, there are numerous magazines you can read.

_____

_____

2.   When ready, take the meat out of the oven immediately.

_____

_____

3.   To work efficiently, frequent oiling of the machine is required.

_____

_____

4. A timid person, every little thing frightened him.

_____

_____

5. After reading the newspapers in the library, they should be put back in their proper place.

_____

_____

6. Meeting her only once, she enchanted him completely.

_____

_____

7. Darkness having come, we stopped for the night.

_____

_____

8. As a child, his parents spoiled him very much.

_____

_____

9. By obeying all traffic regulations, many accidents can be avoided.

_____

_____

10. A comedian at heart, the children were often made to laugh by their teacher.

_____

_____

11. Having painted the outside of the house, the inside should also be painted.

_____

_____

12. The bus being very crowded, we decided to take a taxi.

_____

_____

13. Blowing at sixty miles an hour, the tree was knocked down by the wind.

_____

_____

14. On being notified that the weather would be good, the two men got ready for their long flight.

_____

_____

15. Having been found guilty by the jury, the judge gave the defendant a severe sentence.

_____

_____

2

Adverbial Clauses

Type of Clause	Subordinate Conjunction Beginning the Clause		Sentences
Time	*when*	*as soon as*	I can see you **when** *I finish my work.*
	while	*as long as*	She was reading a book **while** *the dinner was cooking.*
	since	*by the time (that)*	I have not seen him **since** *he returned to the country.*
	before	*now that*	They will leave **before** *you get here.*
	after	*once*	
	until	*as*	Abridgments of time clauses:
			When (or **While**) *young*, I looked at things differently.
			When *a boy*, I looked at things differently.
			She always sings **when** *doing her work*.
			Experience, **when** *dearly bought*, is seldom thrown away.
Place	*where*		We live **where** *the road crosses the river*.
	wherever		Abridgments of place clauses:
			Wherever *possible*, the illustrations are taken from literature.
Cause	*because*		He could not come **because** (or **since, as**) *he was ill.*
	since		**Now that** *he has passed the examination*, he can get his degree.
	as		**Whereas** *they have disobeyed the law*, *they* will be punished.
	now that		**Inasmuch as** *no one was hurt because of his negligence*, the judge
	whereas (legal)		gave him a light sentence.
	inasmuch as (formal)		**On account of** (or **owing to**) **the fact that** *the country was at war*,
	as long as		all the young men were drafted.
	on account of the fact that		
	owing to the fact that		Abridgments of cause clauses:
	in view of the fact that		It is an unpardonable insult, **since** *intentional*.
	because of the fact that		
	due to the fact that (informal)		
Condition	*if*		**If** *it rains*, we won't have the picnic.
	unless		We won't have the picnic **unless** *the weather is good*.
	on condition that		We'll have the picnic **providing that** *it doesn't rain*.

cont. . . .

Type of Clause	Subordinate Conjunction Beginning the Clause	Sentences
	provided } *that* *providing* *in the event that* *in case that* *whether . . . or not*	***In the event*** (or ***in case***) (***that***) *it rains*, the picnic will be post- poned. Abridgments of conditional clauses: In contrary-to-fact conditions: Present—***Were I in your position***, I would take advantage of that offer. Past—***Had I known*** *you were coming*, I would have met you at the station. Please come early ***if possible***. This appliance will not work ***unless*** *properly attached*.
Contrast: concessive	*although* *though* *even though* *even if* *in spite of* } *the fact that* *despite* *notwithstanding (the fact)* *that*	***Although*** (or ***Though***) *I felt very tired*, I tried to finish the work. ***In spite of the fact that*** *prices went down recently*, the company made a huge profit. ***Notwithstanding the fact that*** *the government was weak at that time*, law and order were maintained. Abridgments of concession clauses: ***Although*** *in a hurry*, he stopped to help the boy. ***Although*** *only a boy*, he does a man's work. ***Although*** *fond of his work*, he wants to find a job that will be more challenging.
adversative	*while* *where* (informal) *whereas*	Some people spend their spare time reading, ***while*** *others watch television*.
Purpose	*in order that* *so* (informal) *so that* *for the purpose that*	They climbed higher ***in order that*** *they might get a better view*. He is saving his money ***so that*** *he can go to college*.
Result	*so* + adj. or adv. + *that* *such (a)* + noun + *that* *so that*	She is ***so*** pretty (adj.) ***that she attracts a lot of attention***. She sang ***so*** beautifully (adv.) ***that everyone applauded her performance***. She has ***such*** pretty hair (noun) ***that we all enjoy looking at it***. It's ***such a*** hot day (sing. count. noun) ***that I must go to the beach***. They climbed higher, ***so that*** *they got a better view*.
Comparison	*as* } + adj. or adv. + *as* (*not*) *so* *-er* } + adj. or adv. + *than* *more*	She works just ***as*** hard as *her sister works*. She doesn't work ***so*** (or ***as***) hard ***as her sister works***. She works hard***er than*** *her sister works*. Abridgments of comparison clauses (very common): She works *just ***as*** hard ***as*** her sister (does)*. She works hard***er than*** *her sister (does)*.
Manner	*as if* *as though* especially after *look, seem, act*)	He looks ***as if*** *he needs* (or *needed*) *more sleep*. He hasn't behaved ***as*** *a gentleman should behave*. Abridgment of manner clauses: He hasn't behaved ***as*** *a gentleman should*. He left the room ***as though*** *angry*. The clouds disappeared ***as if*** *by magic*. He raised his hand ***as if*** *to command silence*.

TYPES OF ADVERBIAL CLAUSES

An adverbial clause consists of a subject and predicate introduced by a subordinate conjunction like **when, although, because, if.** Such a clause may be used in initial position, final position, and occasionally in mid-position with the main verb of the sentence. A comma often appears after an introductory clause (especially a long one), but is much less common before a clause in final position. A clause in mid-position must be set off with commas.

Combine the sets of sentences for the following types of adverbial clauses. Replace the italicized expression in the second sentence by a subordinate conjunction in the first sentence. Then note which position each adverbial clause may occupy.

Time—with *when, while, as, before, after, until, since*

EXAMPLE: I was in South America last year.
During this time I learned to speak Spanish.

<u>*While* (or *When*) I was in South America last year, I learned to speak Spanish.</u>

<u>I learned to speak Spanish *while* (or *when*) I was in South America last year.</u>

(Note that there is no comma before this time clause in final position.)

1. John's employer warned him about his careless work.
   From then on John was more careful.

   _____

   _____

2. Edison invented a lamp which conducted electricity.
   Up to this time, gas had been the chief means of lighting homes and streets.

   _____

   _____

3. They moved into an expensive apartment.
   Already they have become very snobbish.

   _____

   _____

4. I was entering the building.
   Just then I saw an old friend of mine.

   _____

   _____

5. They were next door chatting with their neighbors.
   Meanwhile, someone broke into their house and stole their silverware.

   _____

   _____

Contrast

Concessive—with *although, though (less formal), even though*

EXAMPLE: We worked day and night.
Still, we couldn't meet the deadline.
Although we worked day and night, we couldn't meet the deadline.

We couldn't meet the deadline, *although* we worked day and night.

1. She spends a lot of money on clothes.
    Still, they never seem to suit her.

    _____

    _____

2. He was deeply hurt by her remarks.
    However, he said nothing in reply.

    _____

    _____

3. You may not succeed right away.
    But you should keep on trying.

    _____

    _____

Adversative—with *while, where, whereas (formal)*

EXAMPLE: Robert is friendly with everyone.
His brother, *on the contrary*, makes very few friends.
While Robert is friendly with everyone, his brother makes very few friends.[1]

1. The former governor had tried to get the cooperation of the local chiefs.
    The new governor, *on the other hand*, aroused their anger by disregarding their opinions.

    _____

    _____

2. Some newspapers have no advertising at all.
    Others, *on the contrary*, carry many advertisements.

    _____

    _____

3. Some people take pleasure in doing evil.
    Others, *however*, take pleasure in doing good.

    _____

    _____

[1]Adversative clauses are often reversible—**Robert is friendly with everyone, while his brother makes very few friends.**

Cause—with *because, since, as, inasmuch as (formal)*

EXAMPLE: She loved to draw.
For this reason she decided to become a painter.
<u>Because she loved to draw, she decided to become a painter.</u>
<u>She decided to become a painter because she loved to draw.</u>

1. His car was much too small.
This is why he decided to sell it.

_____

_____

2. My assistant is on vacation.
For this reason I have a lot of extra work to do.

_____

_____

3. A number of the conditions in the contract have not been met.
Our company *therefore* has decided to cancel the contract.

_____

_____

4. Hitler believed that the Germans were the master race.
Consequently, he set out to conquer all of Europe.

_____

_____

Condition—with *if, unless, in the event that, provided (that), in case*

EXAMPLE: I might see him.
In this case, I'll invite him to our party tomorrow.
<u>*If* I see him, I'll invite him to our party tomorrow. (Note that the verb in the if clause is in the present tense.</u>
<u>*or* I'll invite him to our party tomorrow if I see him.</u>

1. A robbery might occur in the hotel.
In this case the manager must be notified at once.

_____

_____

2. Perhaps we can get a baby-sitter.
In this case we will go to the theater with you tonight.

_____

_____

3. It might not rain tomorrow.
In this case I'll go to the beach.

_____

_____

4. You must have this leak in the roof fixed.
   Otherwise, the whole ceiling will be ruined.

_____

_____

5. I must get the money on time.
   Otherwise I can't go on my vacation.

_____

_____

ADVERBIAL CLAUSES OF PURPOSE

The adverbial clause is one of three grammatical means of expressing purpose.

	beginning expression:	
Adverbial clause	**so that,** **in order that**	The doctor sent her to the hospital so that she could take a series of tests. (The auxiliary **can, may,** or sometimes **will** is used in the clause. Sequence of tenses is observed after a verb in the past tense.)
Infinitive phrase	**(in order) to**	The doctor sent her to the hospital to take a series of tests.
Prepositional phrase	**for**	The doctor sent her to the hospital for a series of tests.

Use the words in parentheses to form an adverbial clause of purpose. Use the correct auxiliary (**can, may, will**) and the correct tense of the auxiliary. Then see whether you can also make an infinitive phrase and a prepositional phrase.

EXAMPLE: He's buying some wood (he, make, bookcase).

He's buying some wood so that he can make a bookcase.

He's buying some wood to make a bookcase.

He's buying some wood for a bookcase.

1. He went outside (he, get, some fresh air).

_____

2. Please go to the laboratory (you, get, blood test).

_____

3.   He worked part-time (he, support, himself, while attending college).

_____

4.   She went to the post office (she, buy, some special stamps).

_____

5.   They checked the manuscript carefully (they, find, any errors).

_____

6.   Many people save money regularly (they, avoid, be, destitute, in their old age).

_____

7.   He's taking a special course (he, become, real estate broker).

_____

8.   She put up some curtains in the kitchen (she, make, room, look more cheerful).

_____

9.   They were traveling tourist class (they, save, money).

_____

10.   He left the office a little early (he, see, his dentist).

_____

11.   They went to the country (they, have, quiet vacation).

_____

12.   They're working night and day (they finish, job, on schedule).

_____

2-3
VERBS IN TIME CLAUSES
FUTURE TIME

The *present tense* is used in time clauses expressing future time.

He will go straight home after he **closes** the store.
She will never marry until she **finds** the right man.

The present perfect tense may occur in future time clauses, especially with *after* or *until*.

He will go straight home after he **has closed** the store.
She will never marry until she **has found** the right man.

Supply the verb forms for *future time* in the following sentences. (Watch for the position of the time clauses. Some are at the beginning of the sentence; some are at the end.)

EXAMPLE: After they (make) <u>make or have made</u> one more payment on the mortgage, they (own) <u>will own</u> the house.

1. When his boss (fire) _____ him, then he (be)

    _____ sorry he didn't work harder.

2. After the wind (die down) _____, we (go)

    _____ for a long walk.

3. They (check) _____ the weather report tomorrow morning

    before they (go) _____ to the beach.

4. We (have) _____ everything ready by the time you (get)

    _____ here.

5. We (not be) _____ able to have a meeting until one of our

    members (return) _____ from his business trip.

6. When I (see) _____ him next week, I (ask)

    _____ him about that matter.

7. After he (find) _____ the mistake in the figures, he (retype)

    _____ the statistical chart.

8. He (not do) _____ anything until he (see)

    _____ a lawyer.

9. Until you (pay) _____ your current bill, we (not extend)

    _____ you any further credit.

10. They (buy) _____ everything they need before the child (be

    born) _____.

11. Before winter (set in) _____, the heating equipment (be fully

    checked) _____.

12. After I (do) _____ the dishes, we (have)

    _____ a game of cards.

A past **when** clause may be used either with a past continuous action that is interrupted or with an action that has just been completed.

Main Clause	Time Clause
Past progressive I **was shopping** downtown He **was getting** ready for bed (The continuous action is not completed.)	when I **met** an old friend. when the phone **rang.**
Past perfect He **had** just (*or* already, no sooner) **gone** to bed She **had** barely (*or* scarcely) **recovered** from one stroke (The action has just been completed.)	when the phone **rang.** when she **suffered** another.

Occasionally, **just** and **already** occur with either an interrupted continuous action or an action that has just been completed.

1. Interrupted continuous action—**She was just** (or **already**) **clearing the table when a late dinner guest arrived.**
2. Action just completed—**She had just** (or **already**) **cleared the table when a late dinner guest arrived.**

Supply the correct past tense forms. Use the past perfect tense with **just, already, no sooner, scarcely, barely.** (Note also whether the past progressive tense can be used with **just** and **already,** and note the difference in time.)

EXAMPLE: a. He (water) <u>was watering</u> the lawn when it (start) <u>started</u> to rain.

b. She (scarcely finish) <u>had scarcely finished</u> washing the windows when it (start) <u>started</u> to rain.

1. I (make) _____ a left turn when his car

_____ (hit) me.

2. He (barely recover) _____ from his heart attack when he (be)

_____ stricken with pneumonia.

3. He (already walk) _____ out of the house when he (realize)

_____ he had no money with him.

4. Her husband (sleep) _____ soundly when she (go)

_____ into the bedroom to awaken him.

5. The street (just pave) _____ when some children (step)

_____ into the wet pavement.

6. They (live) _____ in England when the war (break out)

_____ .

7. They (scarcely return) _____ from the beach when some un-

expected guests (arrive) _____ .

8. All the best pieces (already sell) _____ by the time we (get)

_____ to the auction.

9. We (take) _____ a trip when my wife (become)

_____ very ill.

10. The Browns (just buy) _____ a new house when Mr. Brown

(transfer) _____ to another city.

11. The rioters (try) _____ to seize the building when the police

(disperse) _____ them with tear gas.

12. She (scarcely finish) _____ one important assignment when

she (give) _____ another.

13. She (clean out) _____ the closets when she (come across)

_____ some old photographs.

2-5
CONDITIONAL CLAUSES WITH *UNLESS*

In many sentences, **unless** is the equivalent of **if . . . not.**

If you *don't* get off my property, I'll call the police.
or *Unless* you get off my property, I'll call the police.

Use **unless** to replace **if . . . not** in the following sentences.

EXAMPLE: If it doesn't stop raining soon, they'll have to cancel the ball game.
Unless it stops raining soon, they'll have to cancel the ball game.

1. If he doesn't study harder, he won't pass the examination.

_____

2. If she doesn't learn to be more courteous, she will never have any friends.

_____

3. If he doesn't get better soon, he may have to drop out of school.

_____

4. We will sue you if we don't get the money by tomorrow.

_____

5. If we don't leave right away we'll miss our bus.

_____

6. If we don't start out now, we won't get there before dark.

_____

7. You'll lose the money if you don't put it in a safe place.

_____

8. If he can't pay cash, they won't sell to him.

_____

9. The strikers won't go back to work if a contract isn't signed.

_____

10. If you don't watch your diet, you may become sick.

_____

11. Don't give this package to him if he doesn't sign a receipt for it.

_____

12. If he doesn't get here soon, we'll have to leave without him.

_____

2-6
REAL CONDITIONS (1)
FUTURE TIME

Real conditions are conditions that are possible to be realized. They often refer to one event in the future.

1. With future main verb—**If the weather *is* good, I'*ll go* to the beach.**
2. With imperative main verb—**If he *calls*, *tell* him to come here at once.**

Usually the present tense is used in the conditional clause. Occasionally **will** occurs in this clause in the sense of **be willing**—**If you *will* clear the table, I'll wash the dishes. Should** may also be found in a real conditional clause with the meaning of *it happens that*—**If he *should* call, tell him I'll be right back.**
The verb in the main clause may also be:

be going to	**If the weather is good, I'm going to go to the beach.**
may or might	**If the weather is good, I may (or might) go to the beach.**
(to express possibility)	

Supply the correct verb forms for future conditions. Note where **should** may also be used in the conditional clauses.

EXAMPLE: a. If they (not get) <u>don't get</u> here soon, we (leave) <u>will leave</u> without them.

   b. If you (need) <u>need (*or* should need)</u> more help, please (ask) <u>ask</u> the superintendent.

1. If you (not understand) _____ this math problem, I (explain)

    _____ it to you.

2. We (take) _____ the train if the weather (be)

    _____ very bad.

3. (Telephone) _____ me at once if you (not find)

    _____ the address.

4. We (not go) _____ skating if you (think)

    _____ the ice is dangerously thin.

5. If you (come) _____ over now, I (give)

    _____ you the money.

6. You (have) _____ enough time to buy the tickets if you

    (leave) _____ half an hour early.

7. If you (see) _____ Robert, (give)

    _____ him my best regards.

8. If you (not drive) _____ more carefully, you (may have)

    _____ an accident.

9. If a customer (want) _____ to see me, (tell)

    _____ him I'll be back in ten minutes.

10. If I (go) _____ to the post office, I (get)

    _____ you some stamps.

11. If you (eat) _____ those green apples, you (may get)

    _____ sick.

2-7
REAL CONDITIONS (2)
GENERAL TIME

Real conditions may be used in general statements about repeated events.

General time (*timeless*)	(Generally) If (*or* when, whenever) the weather **is** good,	**I go** to the beach.
Past time	(Last year) If (*or* when, whenever) the weather **was** good,	**I went** to the beach.

Note that for general time, the *present* tense is used for both clauses; for *past* time, the *past* tense is used for both clauses. Note further that in each sentence **if** may be replaced by **when** or **whenever**.

A. Supply the correct forms for timeless real conditions.

EXAMPLE: If they (have) <u>have</u> money, they (go) <u>go</u> to the theater.

1. If we (go) _____ to their house, we always (bring) _____ a present.

2. If I (sit down) _____ to watch television, I (not notice) _____ how quickly the time passes.

3. If she (have) _____ financial troubles, she (ask) _____ her father to help her.

4. Our cat never (eat) _____ if we (leave) _____ her in the house alone.

5. If he (make) _____ a large sale, he (take) _____ his wife out to an expensive restaurant.

6. If the weather (be) _____ very bad, all the schools (be) _____ closed.

7. Her headache (get) _____ better if she (take) _____ an aspirin.

8. If her husband (not like) _____ her new dress, she (return) _____ it to the store.

9. He (take) _____ a walk in the park if he (have) _____ time.

B. Begin each sentence in A with **last year** and give the verb forms for *past* real conditions.

EXAMPLE: Last year, if they (have) <u>had</u> money, they (go) <u>went</u> to the theater.

2-8
UNREAL CONDITIONS (CONTRARY TO FACT)

Unreal conditions refer to situations that are not happening in the present or have not happened in the past.

Present time	If the weather **were** good now,	I **would go** to the beach.
Past time	If the weather **had been** good yesterday,	I **would have gone** to the beach.

Note that in these sentences, a contrary-to-fact condition exists. In the first sentence, the weather is *not* good now; in the second sentence, the weather was *not* good yesterday.

The past subjunctive form is used with present unreal conditions, the past perfect with past unreal conditions.[2]

Might and **could** may also be used in the main clause.

A. Use the verb form for *present unreal* conditions.

EXAMPLE: If he (study) <u>studied</u> harder, he (pass) <u>would pass</u> his examinations.

1.   If he (love) _____ her, he (not behave)

   _____ so badly.

2.   If he (attend) _____ classes more often, he (be)

   _____ a better student.

3.   I (may speak) _____ English better if I (have)

   _____ more practice.

4.   If I (be) _____ in the library, I (look up)

   _____ that information in the encyclopedia.

5.   If I (have) _____ a lot of money, I (help)

   _____ the poor.

6.   If I (know) _____ more Spanish, I (visit)

   _____ South America.

7.   If I (have) _____ more leisure time, I (take up)

   _____ painting.

8.   She (look) _____ better if she (not use)

   _____ so much makeup.

9.   If it (not be raining) _____ , I (go)

   _____ fishing.

10.   We (can play) _____ tennis if we (have)

   _____ some rackets.

11.   If I (earn) _____ enough money, I (buy)

   _____ a boat.

12.   If I (be) _____ in his place, I (accept)

   _____ the job that was offered him.

[2]These subjunctive forms are the same as the indicative, except that for the verb **be,** only **were** is used for present time in formal usage. Informally, **was** is often heard.

13. I (lend) _____ him money if he really (need)

_____ it.

14. If I (not be) _____ so busy, I (go)

_____ to the movies with you.

B. Use the verb forms for *past unreal* conditions for all the sentences in A.

EXAMPLE: If he (study) <u>had studied</u> harder, he (pass) <u>would have passed</u> his examinations.

2-9
REAL AND UNREAL
CONDITIONAL CLAUSES

Complete the following sentences containing either real or unreal conditional clauses.

1. If I felt better today, _____

2. If you get sick, _____

3. If you had done what I told you, _____

4. If anyone asks for me, _____

5. If anyone insults me, _____

6. If we don't understand our teacher, _____

7. If he exercised more often, _____

8. If we had known you were coming, _____

9. If he had told the truth, _____

10. If we have time, _____

11. If you don't stop talking, _____

12. If we had more money, _____

13. If the world population continues to grow, _____

14. If the fire had spread, _____

1. I would be more patient with him if _____

2. We will wait for you if _____

3. I would not have had any trouble if _____

4. He would be very happy if _____

5. I would have bought that car if _____

6. He would learn English faster if _____

7. They will go to the movies tonight if _____

8. They go to the museum if _____

9 We would have been there by now if _____

10. I never get to work on time if _____

11. We won't finish the work today if _____

12. You should eat less if _____

13. We wouldn't have run out of gas if _____

14. The pollution of the air will get worse if _____

2-10
CONDITIONAL CLAUSES
BEGINNING WITH *WERE, HAD, SHOULD*

In unreal conditions, and in real conditions with **should,** it is possible to omit **if** and reverse the order of the subject and the auxiliary.

If we had known about this sooner,
        or
Had we known about this sooner,   } we could have helped you.

If you should need more money,
        or
Should you need more money,   } I'll be glad to lend you some.

Change the conditional clauses to the forms without **if.**

EXAMPLE: a. If I were in your place, I would ask them for more information.
Were I in your place, I would ask them for more information.

b. If he should come early, tell him to wait for me.
Should he come early, tell him to wait for me.

1. If any packages should be lost, the insurance company must be notified immediately.

_____

_____

2. If I had known about your illness, I would have visited you in the hospital.

_____

_____

3. If there should be any new developments in this case, we'll let you know immediately.

_____

_____

4. If he had taken the advice of his lawyer, he would have saved himself a great deal of trouble.

_____

_____

5. If he were alive today, he would be astonished at all the new buildings that have gone up here.

_____

_____

6. If I had known you were arriving, I would have met you at the airport.

_____

_____

7. If I were able to do so, I would give him the money he needs for the operation.

_____

_____

8. If the meeting should be canceled, let me know immediately.

_____

_____

9. If they had left a little earlier, they would have avoided the heavy traffic.

_____

_____

10. If we should decide to leave earlier, we'll call you.

_____

_____

11. If he had been advised properly, he would not have made such a poor investment.

_____

_____

2-11
MIXED TIME IN UNREAL CONDITIONS

A conditional clause containing a past unreal form may be combined with a main clause containing a present unreal form.

If the boy *had listened* to his parents last year, he *wouldn't be* in trouble now.

He *would be studying* at the university now if his father *hadn't lost* all his money.

Supply the required conditional forms for these sentences that combine past unreal time with present unreal time.

EXAMPLE: He (be) <u>would be</u> dead now if the doctor (not operate) <u>had not operated</u> on him right away.

1. If he (want) _____ to run for office again, he (be) _____ the mayor now.

2. They (still be) _____ missing at sea if a passing freighter (not spot) _____ them.

3. I (be) _____ angry if you (not call) _____ me as soon as you arrived in town.

4. If he (not be) _____ so stubborn, he (now be) _____ our new chairman.

5. If you (come) _____ sooner, you (be) _____ skating with them now.

6. If you (not eat) _____ so much, you (not be) _____ so sleepy now.

7. If she (do) _____ as the doctor told her, she (already be) _____ back at work.

8. They (be) _____ rich now if they (buy) _____ the land when it was offered to them.

9. If the floods (not destroy) _____ their home, they (be) _____ living comfortably now.

10. The children (still be) _____ in the park if their mother (not come) _____ for them.

2-12
UNREAL CONDITIONS
IN SENTENCES WITH *BUT, OR, OTHERWISE*

Unreal conditions may be put in a form that is grammatically coordinate with the main clause. **But, or, otherwise** join such clauses.

1. Present unreal condition—**If I knew his address, I would write him.**

> I would write him, ***but*** I don't know his address.
> I don't know his address, ***or*** I would write him.
> I don't know his address; ***otherwise*** I would write him.

2.   Past unreal condition—**If I had known his address, I would have written him.**

> I would have written him, **but** I didn't know his address.
> I didn't know his address, **or** I would have written him.
> I didn't know his address; **otherwise** I would have written him.

Note that the clauses in such sentences are in positive-negative contrast.

A. Change the unreal conditional clauses to independent clauses after but.

EXAMPLE: a. I would wear my red dress if it didn't have a stain in the front.
<u>I would wear my red dress but it has a stain in the front.</u>

b. We would have arrived sooner if we hadn't had a flat tire.
<u>We would have arrived sooner, but we had a flat tire.</u>

1.   I would call him up if he had a telephone.

_____

2.   I would type this letter if my typewriter were working.

_____

3.   She would have baked more cookies if she hadn't run out of sugar.

_____

4.   She would cut her hair short if she had the courage to do so.

_____

5.   We would be at the beach now if it weren't raining.

_____

6.   We would have met you at the airport if we had known when you were arriving.

_____

_____

7.   I would go to the theater often if I could afford it.

_____

B. Change to sentences containing unreal conditional clauses.

EXAMPLE: a. He would clear the snow, but he can't find the shovel.
<u>He would clear the snow if he could find the shovel.</u>

b. We lost our way, or we would have been here sooner.
<u>If we hadn't lost our way, we would have been here sooner.</u>

c. He didn't come to the meeting last night; otherwise I would have seen him.
<u>If he had come to the meeting last night, I would have seen him.</u>

1. I would have written to you earlier, but I was very busy.

    _____

    _____

2. They didn't realize the consequences of their action, or they wouldn't have done such a thing.

    _____

    _____

3. We don't have any more cameras in stock; otherwise we would fill your order immediately.

    _____

    _____

4. The superintendent didn't have a master key, or he would have unlocked the door for me.

    _____

    _____

5. I would love to go to Hawaii, but I can't afford it.

    _____

    _____

6. I'm very busy this week; otherwise I would certainly come to your party.

    _____

    _____

7. We would serve wine with the dinner, but we don't have any.

    _____

    _____

8. I didn't know the size you wore, or I would have bought you some gloves.

    _____

    _____

9. I would help him, but I don't know how.

    _____

    _____

10. I'm late for an appointment; otherwise I would be glad to have some coffee with you.

    _____

    _____

11. He isn't in town, or he would help you.

    _____

    _____

2-13
ADVERBIAL CLAUSES OF RESULT
WITH *SO*, *SUCH*, *SUCH A*

---

so:	with *adjectives*	The bookkeeper is **so efficient** that his figures never need to be checked.
	with *adverbs*	The bookkeeper works **so efficiently** that his figures never need to be checked.

such (a) with *nouns:*

such a + singular countable nouns	This is **such an ugly chair** that I am going to give it away.
such + plural countable nouns	These are **such ugly chairs** that I am going to give them away.
such + noncountable nouns	This is **such ugly furniture** that I am going to give it away.

But: **so much trouble, so many difficulties**

A. Supply **so, such, such a.**

1. It's _____ warm today that I'm going to the beach.

2. We're _____ pleased with these new towels that we're going to buy some more.

3. He has done _____ foolish things that he will get into serious trouble.

4. He made _____ generous contribution to the university that they are naming one of the new buildings after him.

5. This hedge grows _____ fast that we have to trim it often.

6. We had _____ good time that we hate to leave the party.

7. The thief came in _____ quietly that the sleeping couple never heard him.

8. He is _____ extravagant that all his money is spent long before his next paycheck.

9. Their house was _____ severely damaged by the fire that it will have to be completely rebuilt.

10. He wastes _____ much time watching television that he never finishes his homework.

11. He has read that book _____ many times that he knows it by heart.

12. He's had _____ much trouble with his car that he's decided to sell it.

13. Her work at the university has been _____ poor that she is thinking of leaving.

B. Combine each group of words so that the second group becomes a result clause.

EXAMPLE: beautiful piano   I'm sorry I have to sell it.
<u>This is such a beautiful piano that I'm sorry I have to sell it.</u>

1. lazy boy   he will never amount to anything.

_____

2. delicious food   we ate too much.

_____

3. ran quickly   I'm out of breath.

_____

4. much money   they'll never be able to spend it all.

_____

5. stingy   they never want to eat out.

_____

6. hot climate   all kinds of tropical plants can grow here.

_____

7. boring people   we hate to visit them.

_____

8. much noise   I can't study.

_____

9. crowd in the street   we could hardly move.

_____

10. many children were sick   the school closed down.

_____

11. fine weather   they decided to go for a drive in the country.

_____

2-14
PHRASAL CONJUNCTIONS
IN ADVERBIAL CLAUSES

Replace each phrasal conjunction by a single-word conjunction. (The listing of adverbial clauses at the beginning of this chapter will provide some help for this exercise.)

EXAMPLE: *In spite of the fact that* <u>Although</u> *she was already a grandmother, she looked very young.*

1. *Everywhere that* _____ he went, he was warmly received.

2. *During the time that* _____ I was going to college, I was also working as a waitress on weekends.

3. His wife is suing for divorce *on the grounds that* _____ her husband did not support her and the children.

4. We can only do the job for you *on condition that* _____ the work is paid for in advance.

5. *At the moment when* _____ the bell rang, the students rushed out of the classroom.

6. *Notwithstanding the fact that* _____ their armies had been defeated many times, the morale of the people was quite good.

7. They had a bitter quarrel *on account of the fact that* _____ each one felt he was being cheated.

8. *In the event that* _____ you cannot meet us as planned, please let us know immediately.

9. *Owing to the fact that* _____ the youngsters today feel very uncertain about the future, some of them are taking drugs or running away from home.

10. *Regardless of the fact that* _____ none of his friends thought it was a good idea, he decided to buy a house.

11. *In view of the fact that* _____ we are in great financial distress at the moment, we would appreciate your renewing our loan.

12. *In proportion as* _____ the value of land increased, the taxes on the land were increased.

13. *As long as* _____ the tickets for the show were given to us free, we might as well go to see it *in spite of the fact that* _____ it was badly reviewed by the critics.

2-15
REVIEW OF ADVERBIAL CLAUSES

Combine the following sets of sentences so that the italicized sentence becomes an adverbial clause. (Some introductory words in the second sentence of each group may need to be omitted.)

1. *He had always preferred blondes.*
   He married a brunette.

   _____

   _____

2. *He has always provided for his children.*
   He has never given them any affection.

   _____

   _____

3. Soccer is a popular spectator sport in England.
In the United States it is football that attracts large audiences.

_____

_____

4. They were sitting in the front row.
They wanted to hear every word of the lecture. (use a clause of purpose)

_____

_____

5. *Edison invented a lamp which conducted electricity.*
Up to this time, gas had been the chief means of lighting homes and streets.

_____

_____

6. *They moved into an expensive apartment.*
Already they have become very snobbish.

_____

_____

7. *We finished breakfast.*
Then we went for a walk.

_____

_____

8. *My assistant is on vacation.*
I have a lot of extra work to do.

_____

_____

9. *Hitler believed that the Germans were the master race.*
He set out to conquer all of Europe.

_____

_____

10. *It might not rain tomorrow.*
In this case I'll go to the beach.

_____

_____

11. *He'd better get here soon.*
Otherwise we'll have to leave without him.

_____

_____

12. *You ate too much.*
    Otherwise you wouldn't be so sleepy now.

    _____

    _____

13. I would write to him.
    But I don't have his address.

    _____

    _____

14. I would have bought you some gloves.
    But I didn't know the size you wore.

    _____

    _____

15. *We don't have any more cameras in stock.*
    Otherwise we would fill your order immediately.

    _____

    _____

16. I was watering the lawn.
    It started to rain.

    _____

    _____

17. This is an ugly chair.
    I'm going to give it away. (use a clause of result)

    _____

    _____

18. They are very boring people.
    We hate to visit them. (Use a clause of result)

    _____

    _____

19. They are very stingy.
    They never want to eat out. (use a clause of result)

    _____

    _____

3

Adjective Clauses

Adjective clauses are also called *relative clauses*.

(Pro)noun Antecedent[1] Meaning:	Introductory Word	Illustrative Sentences
1. a person	relative pronoun: **who** (**whom** *or* **whose**) **that**	Introductory word functioning as: *Subject*—He paid the man *who* (*or that*) **had done the** work. *Object of verb*—He paid the man *whom* (*or that*) **he had hired.** *Object of preposition*—He paid the man from *whom* **he had borrowed the money.** *Possessive adjective*—This is the girl *whose* **picture you saw.**
2. a thing	**which** **that**	*Subject*—Here is a book *which* (*or that*) **describes animals.** *Object of verb*—The chair *which* (*or that*) **he broke is being repaired.** *Object of preposition*—She was wearing the coat **for** *which* **she had paid $2,000.**
	relative adverb:	
3. a time	**when**	This is the year *when* **the Olympic Games are held.**
4. a place	**where**	Here is the house *where* **I live.**
5. a reason	**why**	Give me one good reason *why* **you did that.**

Other words that may introduce adjective clauses are:

before *or* **after**	He became sick the day **before** he was to leave for his vacation.
as (after **the same**)	She made the same mistakes **as** (*or* **that**) her sister did.

[1]An *antecedent* is the noun or pronoun before the adjective clause which the clause refers to: **the woman** who wrote the book; **the book** which became a best seller.

PUNCTUATION OF ADJECTIVE CLAUSES

Use Commas (nonrestrictive clauses)		Do Not Use Commas (restrictive clauses)
When the antecedent is restricted in itself:		*When the antecedent is restricted by the adjective clause:*
Antecedent a proper noun	Many people congratulated **William Faulkner,** who had just won the Nobel Prize for literature.	Many people congratulated **the man** who had just won the Nobel Prize for literature.
Antecedent of one of a kind	**The boy's mother,** who loves him very much, has made many sacrifices for his happiness.	**A mother** who loves her son very much will make many sacrifices for his happiness.
Antecedent restricted by the preceding context	Late in the evening they sent out for some coffee. **The coffee,** which had been boiling for a long time, tasted rancid.	**Coffee** which has been boiling for a long time will taste rancid.
When the antecedent refers to **all** *of a class:*		*When the antecedent is limited by the adjective clause to* **some** *of a class:*
	The chairs, which were in bad condition, were sent out to be repaired and refinished. (**All** the chairs were in bad condition and were sent out.)	**The chairs** which were in bad condition were sent out to be repaired and refinished. (Some of the chairs—those in bad condition—were sent out. The remaining chairs were not sent out.)

Note that the clause without the commas (restrictive clause) *distinguishes* one or some from others. If no distinction—or choice—is intended or necessary, a clause with no commas (nonrestrictive clause) is used.

Insert the adjective clause in each of the sentences below. Do not use commas if the adjective clause serves to identify the antecedent or to limit the quantity of the antecedent.

1. **Adjective clause**—who has too great expectations from his son.

   a. Dr. White _____ may be disappointed.

   b. A man _____ may be disappointed.

2. **Adjective clause**—where he keeps his money now.

   a. The bank _____ is a very old and reliable one.

   b. The National Savings Bank _____ is a very old and reliable one.

3. **Adjective clause**—who gave the lecture yesterday

   a. The gentleman _____ is a famous scientist.

   b. Dr. William Johnson _____ is a famous scientist.

4. **Adjective clause**—which revolves around the sun

    a. The earth _____ is called a planet.

    b. A heavenly body _____ is called a planet.

5. **Adjective clause**—who serves as a symbol of nobility and dignity

    a The queen of England _____ is loved by her people.

    b. A queen _____ is loved by her people.

6. **Adjective clause**—who has studied his culinary art in France

    a. The restaurant hired a new cook recently. The cook _____

    _____ is expected to be very good.

    b. A cook _____ is expected to be very good.

7. **Adjective clause**—which has all the latest improvements

    a. An air-conditioner _____ is quite expensive.

    b. An air-conditioner is being installed in the new theater. The air-conditioner

    _____ is quite expensive.

8. **Adjective clause**—which were painted by the great masters of the Renaissance.

    a. Some of the pictures _____

    _____ sold for a high price at the auction. (omit *some of*)

    b. All the pictures _____

    _____ sold for a high price at the auction. (omit *all*)

3-2
CASE OF RELATIVE PRONOUNS
INTRODUCING ADJECTIVE CLAUSES

Relative Pronoun as	Person	Thing
Subject	The doctor **who** (*or* **that**) came to see the sick woman gave her some medicine.	The tree **which** (*or* **that**) was planted last year already has blossoms.
Object of verb	The doctor **whom** (*or* **that**) they had called was delayed because of a traffic accident. *Informal:* The doctor **who** they had called was delayed because of a traffic accident. *or* The doctor they had called. . . .	The tree **which** (*or* **that**) his father planted last year already has blossoms. *Informal: The tree his father planted last year already has blossoms.*

cont. . . .

Relative Pronoun as	Person	Thing
Object of preposition	The doctor to **whom** she sent her friend is a well-known specialist. *Informal:* The doctor **who(m)** she sent her friend to is a well-known specialist. *or* The doctor she sent her friend to is a well-known specialist.	The tree under **which** he is standing is a very old one. *Informal:* The tree **which** (*or that*) he is standing under is a very old one. *or* The tree he is standing under is a very old one.
Possessive	Her doctor, **whose** office was newly decorated, started to charge higher fees.	That tree, the branches **of which** are almost bare now, is a very old one. *Informal:* That tree, **whose** branches are almost bare, is a very old one.[2]

That is used for persons and things in restrictive clauses only.
The relative pronoun may be omitted only in restrictive clauses.

Change the *second sentence* in each group of sentences into an adjective clause and insert in the space in the first sentence. Be careful of the punctuation of the adjective clauses. Observe formal usage, but note where informal choices may be made.

EXAMPLE: The police finally arrested the thieves _____.
They had participated in the great train robbery.
The police finally arrested the thieves who (*or* that) had participated in the great train robbery.

1. The musicians _____

_____ arrived very late because of the storm.
The company had hired them for the office party.

2. The rains _____

_____ came too late to save the crops.
The farmers were expecting them.

3. Abstract art _____

_____ is concerned with esthetic form rather than with graphic representation.
Many people do not understand abstract art.

4. At the flea market she bought a ring _____.
It was supposed to be 200 years old.

[2]Even in formal English, many writers prefer **whose** to the more awkward **of which** phrase.

5. The car _____
_____ was continually being stopped by the cheering
crowds.
The President was riding in the car.

6. The man _____
_____ was reluctant to report the theft to the police.
His money had been stolen.

7. The Browns were greatly impressed by the brilliance of Mr. Jones, the young author
_____.
They had just been introduced to him.

8. Our next-door neighbor _____
moved to another town.
Her husband had recently been transferred.

3-3
RELATIVE PRONOUNS
AS OBJECTS OF PREPOSITIONS

Change the *second sentence* in each group of sentences into an adjective clause and insert it
into the first sentence. Use both the formal and the informal forms of the adjective clause. Be
careful of the punctuation of the clause.

EXAMPLE: a. The company _____ employs many people.
  She works for the company.

  The company for which she works employs many people.

  The company (which *or* that) she works for employs many people.

  b. Prof. Emery _____ has written a very controversial book.
  Everyone is talking about him these days.

  Prof. Emery, about whom everyone is talking these days, has written a very controversial book.

  Prof. Emery, who(m) everyone is talking about these days, has written a very controversial book.

1. The house _____ is very old.
The Taylors live in the house.

_____

_____

2. The fire _____ is now under control.
The Fire Department has been fighting against it for several hours.

_____

_____

3. The bank _____ is very reliable.
I have just borrowed some money from it.

_____

_____

4. My father-in-law _____ is lending me some money for a new house.
I can always depend on him for help.

_____

_____

5. Beethoven's Moonlight Sonata _____ is a great piece of music.
I listen to it whenever I play my records.

_____

_____

6. He has gotten himself into a dangerous situation _____.
He has no control over this situation.

_____

_____

7. The Empire State Building _____ is one of the tallest buildings in the world.
We are just going into this building.

_____

_____

8. The Rocky Mountains _____ are very beautiful.
We will soon be flying over them.

_____

_____

9. He picked up the toy _____.
His son was playing with the toy.

_____

_____

10. The enemies _____ are poverty and injustice.
Every country fights against these enemies.

_____

_____

11. The street _____ is a very busy one.
Our store is located on that street.

_____

_____

3-4
RELATIVE PRONOUNS
PATTERNING LIKE *SOME OF WHICH*
AND *SOME OF WHOM*

A relative pronoun may be in an **of** phrase which is preceded by the word it refers to. This construction is especially common after pronouns of indefinite quantity and after superlatives used as nouns.

> The new students, **some of whom** came from other countries, were required to take a special orientation program.
>
> This nightclub has put on many shows, **the most spectacular of which** is the present one.

This construction may also be used with other types of nouns.

> They decided to see the movie at the Bijou, **the title of which** intrigued them.

In such clauses, **whose** may be an alternative for **of which**—One of his books, the title of which (*or* whose title) escapes me at the moment, tells all about the "lost continent."

In each group of sentences, change the *second sentence* into an adjective clause and insert it in the blank in the first sentence. Use commas for the adjective clause.

EXAMPLE: The toys, _____ were returned to the manufacturer.
Most of them had been damaged in transit.
The toys, most of which had been damaged in transit, were returned to the manufacturer.

1. The members of the band _____

_____ came from all parts of the city.
The majority of them were amateurs.

2. She hurried home to feed her cats. _____

_____.
One of them had just had kittens.

3. The president appointed a special committee _____

_____.
The chairman of the committee was to report to him periodically.

4. Their apartment _____

_____ was one of the most expensive in the building.
The windows of their apartment faced the river.

5. This old book _____

_____ has had a great influence on me.
The author of the book is unknown.

6. The children _____

_____ went to look for something to stand on.
The tallest of them could not reach the shelf where the cookies were.

7. The storekeepers in the neighborhood _____

_____ asked for more police protection.
Several of them had already been robbed.

8. The residents _____

_____ were given help by the Red Cross.
All of their homes had been damaged by the flood.

9. He was put out of business by his many competitors _____

_____.
The most unscrupulous of them had cut prices below cost.

3-5
ADJECTIVE CLAUSES
USED IN DEFINITION

A word is usually defined by first placing it in a class and then stating what makes it different from the other members of its class (differentiae).

Geography—A science (class) *that* deals with the earth and its life. (differentiae)

Define the following words by adding adjective clauses to the class words that are given. Use the dictionary where necessary.

1. **Cannibal**—A human being *who* _____

_____

2. **Euphemism**—An expression *that* _____

_____

3. **Socialism**—A system or condition of society *in which* _____

_____

4. **Atom**—The smallest component of an element *that* _____

_____

5. **Bullfight**—A spectacle *in which* _____

_____

6. **Economics**—A science *that* _____

_____

7. **Demagogue**—A political leader _____

_____

8. **Capitalist**—A person _____

_____

9. **Peninsula**—A body of land _____

_____

3-6
REVIEW
OF ADJECTIVE CLAUSES

Combine the following groups of sentences so that the *second sentence* in each group becomes an adjective clause modifying the italicized word(s) in the first sentence.
Punctuate carefully. Consider all possible forms, both formal and informal, for the introductory words.

Person as Antecedent

1. *Albert Einstein* will always be revered in history.
   He was not only a great scientist but a great human being.

   _____

   _____

2. A *person* meets all his responsibilities.
   Everyone admires such a person. (omit *such*)

   _____

   _____

3. *The student* was highly praised by his teacher.
   The student's composition was read in class.

   _____

   _____

4. *Ellen Peters* is a very prominent lawyer.
   The judge is talking to her at the moment.

   _____

   _____

5. The *woman* is a very prominent lawyer.
   The judge is talking to her at the moment.

   _____

   _____

6. All of *the office workers* were dismissed by the company. (omit *all of*)
   They had gone on strike for higher pay.

   _____

   _____

7. Some of the *office workers* were dismissed by the company. (omit *some of*)
   They had gone on strike for higher pay.

   _____

   _____

8. Suddenly *a man* appeared at the back door.
   She knew the man was wanted by the police.[3]

   _____

   _____

9. *The soldiers on the European front* were overjoyed when they received the news of the armistice.
   Many of them had been on active duty for four years.

   _____

   _____

Thing as Antecedent

10. *Tennis* offers a pleasant means of recreation for young people.
    It can be played by two or four players.

    _____

    _____

11. *His last letter* was lost.
    It was the letter in which he enclosed the check.

    _____

    _____

12. *The books* finally arrived.
    He had sent away for the books.

    _____

    _____

13. *The ABC television program* is very popular with young children.
    Some educators are producing the program.

    _____

    _____

14. Some people do not like *modern art*.
    They believe it is only a random splashing of paint on canvas.

    _____

    _____

[3]In an adjective clause, a phrase like **she knew, he remembers, the people believe** is considered parenthetic and does not affect the form of the introductory pronoun. In this sentence, the introductory relative pronoun is the subject of **was wanted**.

Place as Antecedent (use *where*)

15. *The town* has been very much in the news these days.
     The university is located there.

     _____

     _____

16. *The city* is rich in historical associations.
     Henry James preferred to live there.

     _____

     _____

17. *London* is rich in historical associations.
     Henry James preferred to live there.

     _____

     _____

18. *The garage* is very expensive.
     The executives of the company park their cars there.

     _____

     _____

19. There was a wonderful view from *the hilltop*.
     The hikers had stopped there to have lunch.

     _____

     _____

Time as Antecedent (use *when*)

20. The president will see you on *Saturday*.
     On this day he will have more time to spend with you.

     _____

     _____

21. Most students look forward to *the Christmas holidays*.
     At this time they can relax after months of hard work.

     _____

     _____

22. They generally take a short vacation in *January*.
     In this month there is very little business in their store.

     _____

     _____

4

Noun Clauses

Noun Clause Derived From:	Introductory Conjunction	Function of Clause	Examples
1. a statement **Coffee grows in Brazil.**	that	subject subject after **it** subjective complement object of verb appositive	That[1] **coffee grows in Brazil** is well known to all. It is well known **that coffee grows in Brazil.** My understanding is **that coffee grows in Brazil.** I know **that coffee grows in Brazil.** His belief **that coffee grows in Brazil** is correct.
2. a question a. expecting a *yes* or *no* answer **Will he get the money?**	whether (*or* **not**) *also* if	subject subjective complement object of verb object of preposition	**Whether (or not) he gets the money** doesn't concern me. The question is **whether he will get the money.** Do you know **whether (or if) he will get the money?** We were concerned about **whether he would get the money.**
b. interrogative word question **How will he get the money?**	who what which when where why how	subject subjective complement object of verb object of preposition	**How he gets the money** is his own affair. The question is **how he will get the money.** I don't know **how he will get the money.** We were concerned about **how he would get the money.**
3. a request **Write the letter soon.**	that	object of verb	He suggested **that I write the letter soon.**
4. an exclamation **What a pretty girl she is!**	what how	object of verb object of preposition	I hadn't realized **what a pretty girl she was.** We talked about **what a pretty girl she was.**

[1]The use of **the fact that** (rather than **that**) to introduce a noun clause subject emphasizes the factual nature of the subject.

A noun clause consists of a subject and predicate that functions as a noun. One of its most common functions is as the object of a verb, especially of a verb of speaking or mental activity. If such a verb is in the *past tense*, the verb in the noun clause object takes past form also.

A. Indirect Speech—Noun Clauses from Statements

Present Main Verb (No Sequence of Tenses)	**Past** Main Verb (Sequence of Tenses)
He **says** (that):	He **said** (that):
The train **always arrives late.**	The train **always arrived late.**
The train **is arriving.**	The train **was arriving.**
The train **arrived late.**	The train **had arrived late.**
The train **has just arrived.**	The train **had just arrived.**
The train **will arrive soon.**	The train **would arrive soon.**
The train **may be arriving soon.**	The train **might be arriving soon.**

That is omitted in informal usage. The present tense may be retained in a **that** clause object expressing a generalization. (**He** *said* that the train always *arrives* late.)

No comma precedes or follows a noun clause.

Change to indirect speech. Observe the sequence of tenses in all the verbs in the noun clauses. Make the necessary changes in pronouns.

EXAMPLE:

He said, "I need more time to get ready."

He said that he needed more time to get ready. (Note that there is no comma before **that**.)

1. He said, "They have already finished the work."

_____

2. He said, "Construction on your house will begin as soon as the lumber arrives."

_____

3. The technician said, "The laboratory has already sent in the report."

_____

4. The mechanic said, "Your car is repaired and you can pick it up at the garage at any time."

_____

_____

5. She said, "We are planning a farewell party for our two guests."

_____

6. He said, "I will meet you at the airport whenever you wish."

_____

7. Our visitor said, "It rains a great deal in my country."

_____

8. He said, "The weather is so bad that I won't go out at all."

_____

9. The gardener said, "The bushes should be trimmed once a month."[2]

_____

10. She said, "My parents live too far away for me to visit them often."

_____

B. Indirect Speech
Noun Clauses from Questions

Change to indirect speech. Observe the sequence of tenses and make the necessary changes in pronouns. Use normal subject-verb order in the noun clauses.

EXAMPLE: a. He asked me, "Does the train always arrive late?"
   He asked me whether (*or informal* if) the train always arrived late.

   (Note that there is no comma before **whether** and that there is a period at the end of the sentence.)

   b. He asked me, "Where do you keep your keys?"
   He asked me where I kept my keys.

1. He asked me, "Will the report be ready soon?"

_____

2. He asked me, "Has anyone found the missing dog?"

_____

3. He asked me, "Can you cook?"

_____

4. He asked me, "What color do you want?"

_____

5. He asked me, "How much does this umbrella cost?"

_____

[2]**Should** is already a past form and therefore acceptable here. **Should have trimmed** changes the meaning to an act that was not done.

6. He asked me, "What is your name?"[3]

_____

7. He asked me, "Which block do you live on?"

_____

8. He asked me, "Where is the post office?"

_____

9. He asked me, "Why didn't you answer when I called you?"

_____

10. He asked me, "Who was hurt in the accident?"

_____

11. He asked me, "May anyone enter the contest?"

_____

12. He asked me, "When are they leaving for Chicago?"

_____

13. He asked me, "Is the bus non-stop?"

_____

14. He asked me, "Have you ever been to New York?"

_____

15. He saked me, "Which typewriter do you like better?"

_____

16. He asked me, "Who is that pretty girl?"

_____

17. He asked me, "What time is it?"

_____

18. He asked me, "Whose hat is this?"

_____

19. He asked me, "Whom does the blue umbrella belong to?"

_____

[3]If an interrogative word question contains a form of the independent verb **be** + a (pro)noun subject, the order of subject and verb is reversed in an indirect question.

        question   How late **is** the train?

        indirect question   He asked me how late the train **was.**

20. He asked me, "How long have you been waiting?"

_____

21. He asked me, "Which beach did you go to?"

_____

**4-2
SEQUENCE OF TENSES
IN NOUN CLAUSES (2)**

Change the main verb to the past tense and make the changes in the noun clauses required by
the sequence of tenses.

EXAMPLE: a. He denies that he took the money.
<u>He denied that he had taken (informal, *took*) the money.</u>

          b. She is pretending that she hasn't seen him come into the room.
<u>She was pretending (or pretended) that she hadn't seen him come into the room.</u>

          c. I know that I can do the work if he will give me the chance.
<u>I knew that I could do the work if he would give me the chance.</u>

            (Note that sequence of tenses must be observed even in the dependent clauses within the noun clauses.)

1. We believe that he may take the late train home.

_____

2. I assume that the insurance company will pay me for the damage to my car.

_____

3. I think that the baby is crying.

_____

4. We doubt that they have already left.

_____

5. I suppose that they are out to lunch.

_____

6. Our neighbors are threatening that they will call the police if we continue to play such loud music.

_____

_____

7. I suppose that the secretary who has just been hired will prove to be satisfactory.

_____

_____

8. She is complaining that the doctor is charging too much for the series of treatments he is giving her.

_____

_____

9. He insists that the report he has prepared is based on accurate statistics.

_____

_____

10. I promise that after the ball game is over I will come straight home.

_____

_____

4-3
NOUN CLAUSES OBJECTS
FROM STATEMENTS, QUESTIONS,
EXCLAMATIONS

Change each type of sentence into a noun clause object. Be careful to observe the sequence of tenses after a past main verb. Use a period at the end of the sentence unless the entire sentence is a question.

EXAMPLE: a. The package has arrived.
He said <u>(that) the package had arrived.</u>

b. Can they afford to buy a house?
They wondered <u>whether they could afford to buy a house.</u>

c. What time is it?
I don't know <u>what time it is.</u>

d. What a terrible cold she has!
Did you notice <u>what a terrible cold she had?</u>

1. She can do no wrong.

   She believes _____

2. Will the tickets be expensive?

   He couldn't tell us _____

3. Who is playing the piano?

   She asked _____

4. How noisy this typewriter is!

   I hadn't realized _____

5. May I see you soon?

   Please let me know _____

6. Where is the bus stop?

   Can you tell me _____

7. No one is allowed to enter the building.

   The guard explained _____

8. How far is the airport from here?

   I'll try to find out _____

9. What a wonderful hostess she is!

   No one can ever forget _____

10. He doesn't understand the question.

    He pretended _____

11. Is she wearing her diamond ring?

    I didn't notice _____

12. On which street does he live?

    She asked him _____

13. How late it is!

    I hadn't realized _____

14. Her son is a famous athlete.

    She boasted about[4] _____

15. The dictator makes more promises than he keeps.

    The people were irritated by[4] _____

4-4
NOUN CLAUSES AFTER WISH (1) REFERRING TO PRESENT TIME

After the verb **wish,** a **that** noun clause may refer to present or past time. The introductory **that** is often omitted, especially in informal usage.

Wishes referring to present time are often contrary to fact. The past subjunctive form of the verb is used for such wishes.

> My wife plays the piano.   I wish she **played** better (She doesn't).[5]

[4]**The fact that** must be used with a statement that is made the object of a preposition—**The police are suspicious of** *the fact that* **the safe was not locked at the time of the robbery.**
[5]The verb form used in present contrary-to-fact wishes is the same as in unreal conditions—**If my wife** *played* **better.**

A. Supply the correct form for the following present contrary-to-fact wishes. Omit the introductory **that.**

EXAMPLE: a.   I'm at home now. I wish (be at the beach).

<u>I wish I were at the beach.</u>

(Only the form **were** is used formally for the verb **be**)

b.   That's a beautiful picture. I wish (know how to paint).

<u>I wish I knew how to paint.</u>

c.   Our refrigerator is always breaking down. I wish (can afford to buy a new refrigerator).

<u>I wish I could afford to buy a new refrigerator.</u>

1.   I have black hair. I wish (have red hair).

_____

2.   Our apartment is very noisy. We wish (can move away from here).

_____

3.   They live in a tropical climate now. They wish (live in a more moderate climate).

_____

4.   We have to work on our income taxes tonight. Don't you wish (be able to go to a movie instead)?

_____

5.   It's very cold outside. I wish (be warmer).

_____

6.   She lives in the eastern part of the country. She wishes (live in the West).

_____

7.   It's hard for me to express myself in English. I wish (speak English well).

_____

8.   We are sorry you have to leave now. We wish (be able to stay longer).

_____

9.   Our television set isn't working. I wish (know how to fix it).

_____

10.   It's winter now. I wish (be summer).

_____

11.   It takes me a long time to get to work by bus. I wish (have a car) and (can drive to work).

_____

12.   The cat isn't eating. I wish (know what the matter is).

_____

13.   I couldn't sleep last night. I wish (not have to go to work today).

_____

B. Wishes with WOULD

Wishes with **would** often represent present-to-future time. **Would** leaves open the possibility that the wish could become true in the future.

I wish (that) it would stop raining.   vs. I wish (that) it weren't raining now.
I wish (that) he would study harder.   vs. I wish (that) he studied harder.
                                                          (these are both contrary-to-fact at the present time)

Supply the correct form for the following wishes that are possible to realize. Omit the introductory **that**.

EXAMPLE: a.   He is a nuisance. I wish (go away).
                       <u>I wish he would go away.</u>

                  b.   The radio is too loud. I wish (turn it down).
                       <u>I wish you would turn it down.</u>[6]

1.   His hair is very long. His mother wishes (have it cut).

_____

2.   The stock market keeps going down. I wish (start to go up again).

_____

3.   I like a well-kept home. I wish (my neighbors keep their yard clean).

_____

4.   Our television set isn't working. I wish you (have it fixed).

_____

5.   You're driving too fast. I wish (slow down).

_____

6.   This letter is carelessly done. I wish you (type more carefully).

_____

7.   His wife smokes too much. He wishes (stop smoking).

_____

4-5

NOUN CLAUSES AFTER WISH (2) REFERRING TO PAST TIME

Wishes referring to past time did not become true. Past perfect forms are used in such wishes.

My wife plays the piano.   I wish she **had played** better yesterday (but she didn't).[7]

---

[6] This kind of wish represents a polite request.
[7] The verb form used in past contrary-to-fact wishes is the same as in unreal conditions—If my wife *had played* better.

Supply the correct form for the following past unrealized wishes. Omit the introductory **that**.

EXAMPLE: a. I feel very uncomfortable. I wish (not eat so much).

<u>I wish I had not eaten so much.</u>

b. I don't have enough money. I wish (take more money with me when I left the house.)

<u>I wish I had taken more money with me when I left the house.</u>

1. She lives in the city now. She wishes (never leave the country).

_____

2. This house is too small. I wish (not buy it).

_____

3. We miss our old car. I wish (not be in such a hurry to sell it).

_____

4. I can't come to the meeting. I wish (know about it yesterday).

_____

5. Everyone at the party is dressed so formally. I wish (put on my new suit).

_____

6. I'm catching a cold. I wish (not go out in the rain yesterday).

_____

7. The car is out of gas. I wish (think of getting some before we started our trip).

_____

8. He has undertaken an important task. In a few weeks he will wish (never start it).

_____

9. They are very unhappy in their new country. They wish (not leave their native land).

_____

10. Their TV set always needs repairs. They wish (buy a better set).

_____

4-6
NOUN CLAUSES AFTER WISH
VS UNREAL CONDITIONAL CLAUSES

The same subjunctive form of the verb is used both in contrary-to-fact wishes and in unreal conditions. The time expressed by the wish or the condition may be present or past.

Present

real situation	They don't have a television set now.
wish	They wish **they had a television set now.**
condition	**If they had a television set now,** they would watch all the game shows.

Past

real situation	They didn't have a television set last year.
wish	They wish **they had had a television set last year.**
condition	**If they had had a television set last year,** they would have watched all the game shows.

A. The following sentences give real situations that exist in the present. Referring to these situations, write one sentence containing a *present* contrary-to-fact wish and one sentence containing an unreal condition. Complete the sentence containing the unreal condition.

EXAMPLE: My brother lives so far from here now. (real present situation)
     wish   I wish my brother didn't live so far from here now.
     condition   If my brother didn't live so far from here now, I would visit him more often.

1. I have a cold.

    wish _____

    condition _____

    _____

2. She doesn't know how to speak Spanish.

    wish _____

    condition _____

    _____

3. I don't feel well today.

    wish _____

    condition _____

    _____

4. I'm not the President of my country.[8]

    wish _____

    condition _____

    _____

5. That car costs too much.

    wish _____

    condition _____

    _____

6. He doesn't have a lot of money.

    wish _____

    condition _____

    _____

[8]**Were** is the subjunctive form of the verb **be. Was** is often heard in informal usage.

7.   I don't work with my friend.

wish   _____

condition _____

_____

8.   Not everyone has enough to eat.

wish   _____

condition _____

_____

9.   That book is very expensive.[9]

wish   _____

condition _____

_____

10.   I can't leave work early today.

wish   _____

condition _____

_____

11.   It's raining hard now.

wish   _____

condition _____

_____

12.   The newspaper is full of bad news.

wish   _____

condition _____

_____

13.   Her husband smokes too much.[9]

wish   _____

condition _____

_____

14.   He's not a famous rock singer.

wish   _____

condition _____

_____

[9]**Very,** and **too** often become **so** in contrary-to-fact wishes or conditions.

B. The following sentences give real situations that exist in the past. Referring to these situations, write one sentence containing a *past* contrary-to-fact wish and one containing an unreal condition. Complete the sentence containing the unreal condition.

EXAMPLE: My brother lived so far from here last year.(past real situation)

wish   <u>I wish my brother hadn't lived so far from here last year.</u>

condition   <u>If my brother hadn't lived so far from here last year, I would have visited him more often.</u>

1. I caught a cold yesterday.

   wish   _____

   condition   _____

   _____

2. The storm ruined my garden.

   wish   _____

   condition   _____

   _____

3. I didn't write that best seller.

   wish   _____

   condition   _____

   _____

4. The bad weather held up the departure of our plane.

   wish   _____

   condition   _____

   _____

5. He didn't take care of his books.

   wish   _____

   condition   _____

   _____

6. She didn't see that movie.

   wish   _____

   condition   _____

   _____

7. The dog was barking last night.

   wish   _____

   condition   _____

   _____

8. I lost my wallet at the ball game.

wish _____

condition _____

_____

9. The newspaper wasn't delivered this morning.

wish _____

condition _____

_____

10. She couldn't go to the university when she was young.

wish _____

condition _____

_____

11. Our team lost the game yesterday.

wish _____

condition _____

_____

12. I didn't listen to you.

wish _____

condition _____

_____

13. They couldn't finish the work on time.

wish _____

condition _____

_____

4-7
NOUN CLAUSES
WITH INFINITIVE ABRIDGMENT

Abridgment with infinitives occurs most often with noun clause objects that are derived from questions. The agent in an abridged noun clause object is either:

1. the subject of the main verb

I don't know when to go (= when I should go).

2. the object of the main verb

He told *me* when to go (= when I should go).

Replace the word **this** with an abridged noun clause based on the *second sentence* in each group of sentences.

EXAMPLE: a. We haven't decided *this*.
                When should we hold the dance?
                <u>We haven't decided when to hold the dance.</u>

            b. She is showing the children *this*.
                How should they draw a tree?
                <u>She is showing the children how to draw a tree.</u>

1.   I can't remember *this*.
     How can I start your car?

_____

2.   We must find out *this*.
     Where should we deliver these packages?

_____

3.   I have forgotten *this*.
     Which road should I take to get to the lake?

_____

4.   I can't decide *this*.
     Should I go to the movies or should I stay home and watch television?

_____

5.   Please tell me *this*.
     What should I buy and where should I buy it?

_____

6.   The office manager will explain *this* to the new typist. (Put *to the new typist* before the noun clause.)
     Where should she work and what should she do?

_____

7.   I don't know *this*.
     Whom should I see about my taxes?

_____

8.   The committee must decide *this* soon.
     When should it have its next meeting?

_____

9.   I don't know *this*.
     Should I buy the red dress or the blue one?

_____

10.   We must decide *this*.
     Where shall we put all the new furniture?

_____

11. We will soon let you know *this*.
    Where should you deliver the merchandise?

_____

12. She asked the doctor *this*.
    When should I change the bandages?

_____

13. They are considering *this*.
    Should they buy a new car.

_____

4-8
THAT CLAUSES
AFTER VERBS OF URGENCY

That clauses after verbs like **suggest, require, urge** require the simple form of the verb (present subjunctive). This simple form is used regardless of the tense of the main verb.

$$\text{The committee} \left\{ \begin{array}{l} \text{suggests} \\ \text{suggested} \\ \text{has suggested} \\ \text{had suggested} \\ \text{will suggest} \end{array} \right\} \text{that} \left\{ \begin{array}{l} \text{we } \textbf{hold} \text{ more meetings.} \\ \text{everything } \textbf{be} \text{ prepared in advance.} \\ \text{he not } \textbf{give} \text{ the report.} \end{array} \right.$$

Note that such clauses are made negative by the use of **not** before the verb.

Verbs that are followed by **that** clauses with the simple form of the verb are: **advise, ask, beg, command, demand, desire, insist, propose, recommend, request, require, suggest, urge.**

In some clauses after these verbs, **that** may be omitted informally, especially in clauses with pronoun subjects—**The committee suggests we hold more meetings.**

Except in **that** clauses after verbs of strong urgency like **command, demand,** less formal usage permits the auxiliary **should** to accompany the verb—**The committe suggests that we should hold more meetings.**

A. Replace the word **this** by a **that** clause made from the *second sentence* in each group. Use the simple form of the verb in the **that** clause. Note which **that** clauses may also be used with **should.**

EXAMPLE: The law requires *this*.
Everyone must take a test for a driver's license.
<u>The law requires that everyone take a test for a driver's license.</u>

1. The lawyer advised *this*.
   He should sue his tenant for back payment of rent.

_____

2. Her mother insists on *this*. (omit *on*)
   She has to be back home by midnight.

_____

3. The stockbroker has recommended *this*.
   They should not buy that particular stock now.

   _____

4. Her employer demands *this*.
   She must come to work on time.

   _____

5. The committee proposed *this*.
   A lawyer should be consulted regarding their legal rights.

   _____

6. We strongly urge *this*.
   You should not interfere in this matter.

   _____

7. May I ask *this* of you? (omit *of*)
   Do not tell anyone about our plans.

   _____

8. The doctor has suggested *this*.
   The patient should take a long vacation.

   _____

9. I urge *this*.
   Stay in bed until you are over your cold.

   _____

10. The students request *this*.
    They should be given less homework.

    _____

11. The general commanded *this*.
    All the men in the post should be prepared for an immediate attack.

    _____

12. We desire *this*.
    The tour leader should notify us immediately of any change in plans.

    _____

After many of these verbs of urgency, infinitive phrases may provide less formal alternatives for **that** clauses.

The law requires everyone to take a test for a driver's license.

This choice is especially possible for the verbs **advise, ask, command, desire, request, require, urge.**

B. Go over the sentences you have made in A to see which **that** clauses can have alternate forms with infinitive phrases.

THAT CLAUSES
AFTER ADJECTIVES OF URGENCY

The simple form of the verb is used in **that** clauses after adjectives of urgency or advisability.

It is important that each student fill out a registration form.

Among these adjectives are **advisable, desirable, essential, good** (or **better, best**), **imperative, important, mandatory, necessary, requisite, urgent, vital.**
The auxiliary **should** may be contained within the **that** clause after an adjective of urgency—**It is important that each student should fill out a registration form.**

Combine the following groups of sentences so that the *second sentence* becomes a **that** clause after anticipatory **it**. Use the simple form of the verb for this exercise.

EXAMPLE: a. This is essential.
            You should see your dentist at once.
            It is essential that you see your dentist at once.

          b. This is imperative.
            Do not smoke while you are near the gasoline tanks.
            It is imperative that you not smoke while you are near the gasoline tanks.

1. This is necessary.
    You must bring a notebook to class with you every day.

_____

2. This is urgent.
    The police must be notified about those strange phone calls.

_____

3. This is best.
    Cancel your trip at once.

_____

4. This is essential.
    Do not write checks for more money than you have in your account.

_____

5. This is important.
    No one should say anything to him.

_____

6. This is advisable.
    Do not eat any citrus foods because you are allergic to them.

_____

7. This is vital.
   Do not permit our competitors to know our plans.

_____

8. This is desirable.
   The course in general science should be taken before the chemistry course.

_____

9. This is imperative.
   Get your passport renewed before you leave the country.

_____

4-10
REVIEW OF NOUN CLAUSES

Replace the word **this** in one sentence with a noun clause formed from the other italicized sentence. Consider possible choices.

Noun Clauses from Statements

1. He told me *this*.
   "I'm going to get married soon."

_____

2. *Women should have the same opportunities as men.*
   Her husband believes *this*.

_____

3. *We will have peace in the near future.*
   This seems very doubtful.

_____

4. *A broken mirror will bring seven years bad luck.*
   This is a popular superstition.

_____

5. *He doesn't really try.*
   This seems quite clear.

_____

Noun Clauses from Questions

Use normal word order for the noun clauses.

A. From Yes-No Questions

6. *"Did you lock the front door?"*
   Mr. Jones's wife asked him *this*.

_____

7. *Is he a rich man?*
    This is not known even to his relatives.

_____

8. *Will the audience laugh at the new clown?*
    We talked about *this*.

_____

B. From Interrogative Word Questions

9. *Where were you born?*
    I would like to know *this*.

_____

10. *Why did you leave your wife?*
    This will never be understood by your friends.

_____

11. *Whom should we invite to the party?*
    We were wondering about *this*.

_____

Noun Clauses from Exclamations

12. *How hot it is!*
    I'm surprised at *this*.

_____

13. *What a terrible thing hunger is!*
    Few people who have not been hungry can realize *this*.

_____

14. *What bad manners he has!*
    We remarked about *this*.

_____

Noun Clauses from Requests

15. Our teacher suggested *this*.
    Learn the noun clauses as soon as possible.

_____

16. The chairman recommended *this*.
    The meeting should not last more than two hours.

_____

17. Her employer urged *this*.
     Be more careful with your typing.

_____

18. The general commanded *this*.
     All the men were to remain on their posts until further notice.

_____

5

Participial Phrases

Participial Phrase Modifying a Noun or Pronoun	Restrictive Phrase (Narrows Down the Reference of a Noun or Pronoun)	Nonrestrictive Phrase (Does Not Narrow Down the Reference of a Noun or Pronoun)
Position of Participle: *After the noun being modified* a. noun as subject	The girl **talking to the teacher is** very intelligent.	The new President, **supported by all the people,** felt confident about the future.
b. noun as complement of verb	The person to see is that girl **talking to the teacher.**	This is a good government, **supported by all the people.**
c. noun as object of verb	Bob knows the girl **talking to the teacher.**	They now have a good government, **supported by all the people.**
d. noun as object of preposition	Bob is interested in the girl **talking to the teacher.**	They long for a good government, **supported by all the people.**
At the beginning of the sentence (modifying the subject)		**Supported by all the people,** the new President felt confident about the future.
At the end of the sentence (modifying the subject)		The new President felt confident about the future, **knowing that he had the support of all the people.**
Participial Phrase as Part of the Object of a Verb	I heard him **talking to the teacher.**	

FORMS OF PARTICIPLES (1)

	Active Voice		Passive Voice	
		Progressive		*Progressive*
General form (timeless)	**offering** (present participle)		**offered** (past participle)	**being offered**
Perfect form (past time)	**having offered**	**having been offering**	**having been offered**	

Participles are made negative by placing **not** before them—**not offering, not having offered.**

Rewrite the sentences, changing the adjective clauses to participial phrases. Use the required form of the participles. Keep the commas if they are used with the adjective clauses.

Present Participle (example, *offering*)

The time of the main verb determines the time of the participle.

EXAMPLE: a. The woman who is washing the dishes is our new cook.
           The woman washing the dishes is our new cook. (The participle is derived from a progressive verb.)

           b. Anyone who violates this law will be punished.
           Anyone violating this law will be punished. (The participle is derived from a nonprogressive verb.)

1. The gentleman who is crossing the street is an old friend of my father's.

_____

2. Anyone who travels in a foreign country should make sure that he has the proper documents.

_____

3. All passengers who are not going to Rockaway must change trains at the next stop.

_____

4. We need a room which seats one hundred people.

_____

5. Anyone who doesn't enter the country legally will be immediately deported to the country he came from.

_____

6. The young woman, who was running to catch the bus, stumbled and fell.

_____

Past Participle (example, *offered*)

The time of the main verb determines the time of the participle. With most verbs, the past participle has *passive* force.

EXAMPLE: Doctors often recommend rabies shots for anyone who is bitten by a strange dog.

Doctors often recommend rabies shots for anyone bitten by a strange dog.

1. The jewelry which was stolen from our neighbor's house was found by the police.

_____

_____

2. A letter which is sent by airmail should arrive sooner than one which is sent by regular mail.

_____

_____

3. We will prosecute anyone who is caught trespassing on this property.

_____

_____

4. Mr. X, who has been exiled from his homeland for many years, began to make inquiries about whether he could return.

_____

_____

5. The young violinist, who was encouraged by his teacher, decided to enter his name in the music contest.

_____

_____

6. Any package which is not wrapped properly will not be accepted by the post office.

_____

_____

Progressive Passive Participle (example, *being offered*)

This participle expresses present action.

EXAMPLE: Those houses which are now being torn down were built fifty years ago.

Those houses being torn down now were built fifty years ago.

1. The music which is being played now is by Bach.

_____

2. The tooth that is being extracted by the dentist has been hurting me for some time.

_____

3. They expect to help the poor with the money that is being collected.

_____

4. The air conditioner which is now being installed should make the room more comfortable.

_____

5. The letter which is being typed now will introduce you to our representative in London.

_____

Perfect Participial Forms
(examples, *having offered,*
having been offering,
having been offered)

     The perfect forms indicate time that corresponds to the present perfect or the past perfect tense. (Informally the general forms of the participle may also be used in many sentences.)

EXAMPLE: Anyone who has talked to him once will be convinced of his innocence.

             Anyone having talked to him once will be convinced of his innocence.

1. The Smiths, who had found just the house they wanted to buy, began to bargain with the owners to reduce the price.

_____

2. Mr. Preston, who had been offered a good job out-of-town, told his wife they would have to move.

_____

3. The orchestra members, who had been practicing all day, were very tired by evening.

_____

4. Anyone who has served a term in prison will not be hired by that company.

_____

5. Mr. Richards, who had been badly wounded in the last war, was receiving a pension from the government.

_____

6. My brother, who had not understood the chemistry lectures at all, failed the examination.

_____

7. The garden, which had been neglected by the former tenants, was overgrown with weeds.

_____

5-2

FORMS OF PARTICIPLES (2)

Rewrite the sentences, changing the adjective clauses to participial phrases by using one of the participial forms given in 5-1. (Keep the commas if they are used with the adjective clauses.) Note the informal alternatives.

1. The girl who is making the most noise is my daughter.

   _____

   _____

2. The leaflets which were printed last week will be distributed at tonight's meeting.

   _____

   _____

3. The general, who had been warned of the enemy's approaching attack, had all his men ready.

   _____

   _____

4. The movement, which was doomed from the beginning, came to a very inauspicious end.

   _____

   _____

5. The children, who had been instructed not to stay out too long, came back before dinner time.

   _____

   _____

6. The snow which is falling on the highway will make the roads icy by nightfall.

   _____

   _____

7. The children who were swimming too far from shore were ordered back by the lifeguards.

   _____

   _____

8. The money which was not accounted for in his will was distributed equally among his children.

   _____

   _____

9. The men, who were surrounded on all sides by the enemy, had to surrender.

   _____

   _____

10. The patient, who had been advised by his doctor to stop smoking, made every effort to do so.

    _____

    _____

11. Many people who live in large cities are very lonely.

    _____

    _____

12. The dinner which is being prepared now is for the members of the conference.

_____

_____

13. All the guests who are not leaving the hotel tomorrow must let the management know at once.

_____

_____

14. Any student who does not pass the swimming test will not get credit for this course.

_____

_____

5-3
PUNCTUATION AND POSITION
OF PARTICIPIAL PHRASES

Participial phrases that appear after the nouns they modify are punctuated in the same way as adjective clauses, depending on whether the phrase is restrictive (narrows down the reference) or nonrestrictive (does not narrow down the reference).

1. Restrictive—**A student** *hoping to finish college in three years* **must work very hard.** (No commas are used. The class word *student* is narrowed down by *hoping to finish college in three years*.)

2. Nonrestrictive—**Robert,** *hoping to finish college in three years,* **worked very hard.** (Commas are used. **Robert,** which is a proper noun, is already narrowed down to **one** student.)

A. Insert the participial phrases in the blank spaces. Do not use commas if the participial phrases identify the words they refer to, or narrow down their reference.

1. *Participial phrase*—taking a walk in the woods

   a. A person _____
      can see a great variety of birds.

   b. Our botany class _____
      saw a great variety of birds.

2. *Participial phrase*—sitting in the rear of the lecture hall

   a. Oliver and his friends _____
      could not hear the professor.

   b. The students _____
      could not hear the professor.

3. *Participial phrase*—feeling tired

   a. Any of the swimmers _____
      should start to come back to shore.

    b. One of the swimmers _____
started to come back to shore.

4. *Participial phrase*—having achieved success early in life

    a. A person _____
may become bored with life.

    b. My best friend _____
became very bored with life.

5. *Participial phrase*—not satisfied with the service in the store

    a. Mrs. Johnson _____
complained to the management.

    b. Any customer _____
may complain to the management.

6. *Participial phrase*—living a life of great luxury

    a. People _____
are often heedless of the suffering of the poor.

    b. The millionaire's son _____
was often heedless of the suffering of the poor.

7. *Participial phrase*—much admired by women

    a. The handsome actor _____
became very vain and arrogant.

    b. A man _____
may become very vain and arrogant.

8. *Participial phrase*—getting to the concert hall late

    a. The Browns _____
had to wait until the first number was over before they could be seated.

    b. Anyone _____
will have to wait until the first number is over before he can be seated.

9. *Participial phrase*—spoiled by his parents

    a. Their eldest son _____
never became a mature, responsible adult.

    b. A boy _____
may never become a mature, responsible adult.

Nonrestrictive participial phrases may also appear in initial, or less commonly, in final position.

    1. Initial position—*Hoping to finish college in three years*, Robert worked very hard.
    2. Final position—**Robert worked very hard**, *hoping to finish college in three years.*

B. Go over the sentences you have made in A and see which nonrestrictive participial phrases may be moved to initial and final position.

PARTICIPIAL PHRASES IN TWO-PART OBJECTS OF VERBS

Some verbs are followed by two-part objects, the second of which is a participial phrase.

Catch, Keep
Leave, Send, Find

> The police caught ***the young boy stealing a car.***
> They found ***the horse tied to a tree.***

These verbs may be passive—**Their rowboat was found drifting in the lake.**

Verbs of Perception
Behold (Literary), Feel, Hear, Listen to,
Notice, Observe, Overhear,
See, Watch, Witness

> We heard **the children crying.**
> I saw **them running across the street.**

After such verbs of perception, **to**-less infinitives may be alternatives for participial phrases.

> We heard the children **cry.**
> I saw them **run** across the street.

The *to*-less infinitive stresses an action as a whole; the participial form stresses the duration of an action.

Rewrite the sentences, changing the words in parentheses into participial phrases. Note which participles may alternate with **to**-less infinitives.

EXAMPLE: a. The official kept (we, wait, several hours).
            <u>The official kept us waiting (for) several hours.</u>

          b. We watched (children, play, schoolyard).
            <u>We watched the children playing in the schoolyard.</u>
            also <u>We watched the children play in the schoolyard.</u>

1. She felt (her youth, rapidly, slip away).

_____

2. We heard (angry voices, come, next room).

_____

3. She caught (her daughter, take, money, her purse).

---

4. They kept (dog, tie up, yard).

---

5. At the airport we can see (tourists, come, go, all day long).

---

6. He had never before observed (rainbow, arch, sky).

---

7. He listened sleepily (his teacher, explain, lesson).

---

8. You can find (they, have, snack, cafeteria).

---

9. I saw (he, walk, the telephone booth).

---

10. They kept (passengers, wait, half an hour) while the plane was searched for a bomb.

---

11. I overheard (he, reprimand, his salesclerk, the mistake).

---

12. We watched (kitten, try, climb, tree).

---

13. The bandits left (their victims, strand, desert).

---

14. He observed (man, enter, building, stealthily).

---

15. The strong wind sent (his papers, fly, all over the room).

5-5
PARTICIPIAL PHRASES
TO EXPRESS MEANS OR MANNER

Participial phrases used in final position may express means or manner with respect to the subject.

She caught cold sitting on the wet grass.

By sometimes precedes the participle—**She caught cold by sitting on the wet grass.** Participial phrases of manner are especially common after **sit, stand, lie.**

He sat there staring at the wall.

Use the words in parentheses to form a participial phrase of means or manner. Note where **by** may appear before the participle.

EXAMPLE: a. The boy tore his clothes (climb, trees).
   The boy tore his clothes climbing trees.

   b. He earns a living (drive, truck).
   He earns a living (by) driving a truck.

1. He's standing at the corner (watch, girls, go by).

_____

2. All night long he lay awake (think, his financial problems).

_____

3. We spent the whole evening (watch, movies of our hosts' trip to Africa).

_____

4. He sits around all day (do, nothing).

_____

5. The injured man lay on the ground (bleed, profusely).

_____

6. The men amused themselves (tell, stories, the biggest fish they had ever caught).

_____

7. Some men were sitting in the patio (drink, beer).

_____

8. He goes around (look, a bum).

_____

9. He's standing near the window (watch, beautiful sunset).

_____

10. He fell asleep (think, her).

_____

11. He drove around the block (look, place to park).

_____

12.   The Moslem pray (kneel, rug, and face, direction of Mecca).

---

13.   She wore herself out (try, pacify, child).

5-6

PARTICIPIAL PHRASES AS ALTERNATIVES
FOR ADVERBIAL CLAUSES

Like adverbial clauses, participial phrases may indicate *time* or *cause*. Such participial phrases are more likely to occur in initial position than in final position.

Time	Cause
1. *After* **Having finished all her housework,** she sat down to watch television.	**Having worked hard all his life,** he decided to take a long vacation.
2. *While* or *when* **Walking along the street,** I met a friend whom I had not seen for a long time.	

After and **because** may be implied simultaneously in a participial phrase—**Having eaten too much, he became sleepy.**

The time word may also be placed before the participial phrase—**after having finished all her housework; while walking along the street.**[1]

A. Expand the participial phrases into adverbial clauses. Note which participial forms may also have a time word placed before them.

EXAMPLE: a.   Having shopped all day, she was glad to get home and rest.
<u>After she had shopped all day, she was glad to get home and rest.</u>

(*also* After shopping all day. . . . *or* After having shopped all day . . .)

b.   Playing golf in the afternoon heat, he suffered a sunstroke.
<u>While he was playing golf in the afternoon heat, he suffered a sunstroke.</u>

(*also* While playing golf in the afternoon heat. . . .)

[1]Technically, because **after** may be a preposition as well as a conjunction, **having finished** may be considered its gerund object (see Gerund Phrases). **While,** on the other hand, is only a conjunction that introduces adverbial clauses, so **while walking along the street** may be interpreted as an adverbial clause abridged from **while they were walking along the street.**

1. Opening up her jewelry box, she found her diamond rings gone.

_____

2. Believing he was a total failure in everything he did, the man was on the point of suicide.

_____

3. Driving along an almost deserted country road, they ran out of gas.

_____

4. Putting on her hat and coat quickly, she ran outside to see what was causing such a commotion.

_____

5. Not wanting to accept welfare assistance, they often went without food.

_____

6. Depressed by the news she had received, she took a tranquilizer to quiet her nerves.

_____

7. Talking things over, they agreed never to quarrel again.

_____

8. Respecting her parents' wishes, she always came home before midnight.

_____

B. Change the adverbial clauses of time or cause to participial phrases. Note which participial forms may be preceded by time words.

EXAMPLE: a. Because they were impressed by the young man's qualifications, they offered him a good job with their firm.

           Impressed by the young man's qualifications, they offered him a good job with their firm.

      b. While he was walking in the park, he suddenly had a heart attack.

           Walking in the park, he suddenly had a heart attack.

           (*also* While walking in the park. . . .)

1. Because he had been defeated three times in a row, the boxer decided to give up fighting.

_____

2. Because they found no one at home, they left a note saying they had called.

_____

3. When they arrived home late at night, they found that the house had been broken into.

_____

4. While he was backing out of his garage, he hit a dog.

_____

5. Because he was strongly influenced by his young friends, the boy dropped out of school for a while.

_____

6. While they were saying their final goodbyes, the soldiers sadly boarded the train.

_____

7. Because he played tennis every day, he soon became an expert player.

_____

8. Because she didn't know that her husband had already contributed, she gave a large sum of money to the Red Cross.

_____

_____

5-7
INSTRUCTIONS
WITH *HAVE* + PAST PARTICIPLE

Instructions for performing a service may be referred to in the active or passive voice with **have**.

Active—With *to*-less Infinitive	Passive—With Past Participle
I **had** the painter **paint** my house last year.	I **had** my house **painted** last year.
He **had** the tailor **alter** his suit.	He **had** his suit **altered**.
We **had** the store **deliver** the packages.	We **had** the packages **delivered**.

A. Change the instructions after **have** from active to passive. Omit the agent that carries out the instructions. Keep in mind that the passive begins with the *object* in the active sentence.

EXAMPLE: She had the maid wax the floors.
           <u>She had the floors waxed.</u>

1. They had the plumber repair the broken pipe.

_____

2. She had the dressmaker shorten her dress.

_____

3. They are going to have the serviceman install an air conditioner tomorrow.

_____

4. He had his secretary type a dozen letters.

_____

5. We should have the gardener spray the lawn with insecticide.

_____

6. They had the upholsterer reupholster their living room set.

_____

7. They plan to have a contractor build a swimming pool.

_____

8. I had the dry cleaner clean a few dresses.

_____

9. He always has someone make his shirts to order.

_____

10. I had the dentist clean my teeth.

_____

11. She is having the store deliver her groceries.

_____

12. The company is having someone check the applicant's references.

_____

13. The library had someone rebind the worn books.

_____

14. He insists on having everyone obey his orders without question.

_____

B. The following exercise indicates the person who performs a service and the request for the service. Write sentences beginning with **I had** and ending with the service expressed *once as active* and *once as passive.* For the passive, the **by** phrase may be omitted.

Performer of the service	*Request for the service*
EXAMPLE: gardener	Please water the lawn.

I had the gardener water the lawn.

I had the lawn watered (by the gardener).

1. barber   Please cut my hair short.

_____

_____

2. secretary   Would you mind typing a letter?

_____

_____

3. mechanic   The oil in my car needs to be changed.

_____

_____

4. artist   Could you paint my portrait?

_____

_____

5. pharmacist   I would like to renew my prescription.

_____

_____

6. florist   Please deliver the flowers for the party early in the evening.

_____

_____

7. butcher   Would you mind trimming the fat off the meat?

_____

_____

8. cook   Would you please make enough chili for ten people.

_____

_____

9. shoemaker   I'd like you to resole my shoes.

_____

_____

10. plumber   Would you please repair the leaking faucet.

_____

_____

11. bank teller   Could you please cash my check.

_____

_____

12. dentist   I'd like you to X-ray my teeth.

_____

_____

Combine the following groups of sentences so that the *second sentence* becomes a participial phrase referring to the italicized word(s) in the first sentence.

Restrictive Phrases

Do not use commas.

EXAMPLE: *The girl* is waiting for a bus.
 She is standing on the corner.
 The girl standing on the corner is waiting for a bus.

1.   My boss spoke to *the man*.
 The man was applying for a job.

_____

2.   The police opened fire on *the refugees*.
 The refugees were seeking to cross the frontier.

_____

3.   Some *people* should not throw stones. (omit *some*)
 These people live in glass houses.

_____

4.   *A man* will deliver the package to you.
 He will be wearing a dark brown suit.

_____

5.   We are going to use *the money* for medical research.
 The money was collected from the school children.

_____

Nonrestrictive Phrases

Use commas. Note the possible positions of the participial phrases.

6.   *I* took a taxi.
 I was very late for work.

_____

7.   *John* decided to take a long vacation.
 He felt run down and discouraged.

_____

8. *His wife* was always afraid to drive.
   She had never learned properly.

_____

9. *The foreign students* didn't know how to answer the questions.
   They were surprised at the way the questions were put.

_____

10. *The boat* began to sink.
    It was broken in two by the storm.

_____

11. *The students* complained that the test was too hard.
    They had all done poorly on the final examination.

_____

Participial Phrases
as Part of the Object of a Verb

Do not use commas.

12. We watched *the horses*.
    They were running around the track.

_____

13. The soldiers saw *the enemy line*.
    It retreated slowly under the heavy fire.

_____

14. I felt *the earth*.
    It was shaking under me.

_____

15. Everyone ran out to hear *the announcement*.
    It was being broadcast in the street.

_____

6

Gerund Phrases

Gerund phrases perform the same functions as nouns do.

Subject of verb	**Her watering the plants every day** is not necessary.
Object of verb	Her mother appreciates **her watering the plants every day.**
Object of preposition: in prepositional object	Her mother insists on **her watering the plants every day.**
in adverbial phrase	**By watering the plants every day,** she is pleasing her mother.
Subjective complement (predicate noun)	What her mother insists on is **her watering the plants every day.**
Appositive	Her mother insists on one thing— **her watering the plants every day.**

6-1
FORMS OF GERUNDS

Gerunds are participial forms used in noun function. All forms of the participle may be used except the past participle. Like the participle, the gerund may be made negative by placing **not** before it.

A. General (Timeless) Forms

Present participle—**offering**
Passive progressive—**being offered**

These forms express present, past or future time, depending on the time of the main verb.

Supply the active or passive gerund form of the verb in parentheses.

EXAMPLE: a.   (Be) <u>Being</u> honest at all times is not always easy.

b.   The aging couple are counting on (help) <u>being helped</u> financially by their children.

c.   The boy was fired for (not come) <u>not coming</u> to work on time.

1.   (Tell) _____ a little white lie is sometimes preferable to (tell)

_____ the actual truth.

2.   Special forms are required for (record) _____ that information.

3.   He doesn't like (drive) _____ to work; he prefers (take)

_____ the bus.

4.   He denies (have) _____ anything to do with the accused man.

5.   After (interview) _____ for the job, you will be required to take an aptitude test.

6.   On (notify) _____ that he had won a large sum of money in the sweepstakes, he couldn't believe his good fortune.

7.   I don't enjoy (shop) _____ in crowded stores.

8.   He won't tolerate (tell) _____ what to do.

9.   My uncle, who is a lawyer, has often dreamed about (make)

_____ a judge.

10.   (Not do) _____ one's work properly may be worse than (not

do) _____ it at all.

11.   Please refrain from (smoke) _____ in this vehicle.

12.   I am used to (eat) _____ a substantial breakfast in the morning.

B. Perfect Forms (Past Time)

Active—**having offered, having been offering**
Passive—**having been offered**

These forms emphasize the completion of one event before another. In most cases, the general forms are also possible.

Supply the perfect active or passive form of the verb in parentheses. Note also where the general timeless forms may be used.

EXAMPLE: a. I seem to remember (do) <u>having done</u> this exercise before. (also, <u>doing</u>)

  b. After (clear) <u>having been cleared</u> through customs, he immediately took a taxi to his hotel. (also, <u>being cleared</u>)

1. She reproached her husband for (not, tell) _____ her about his business losses.

2. His (marry) _____ twice before made her hesitate about accepting his marriage proposal.

3. Your (help) _____ us when we were in trouble will never be forgotton.

4. After (just recover) _____ from his long illness, the unfortunate man was hit by a car.

5. We appreciated (have) _____ this opportunity to visit with you.

6. After his holiday was all over, he regretted (spend) _____ so much money for so little pleasure.

7. I can't understand his (not call) _____ me while he was in town.

8. He received a substantial raise for (find) _____ a more efficient way of manufacturing the company's product.

9. His (be) _____ in prison made it hard for him to get a job.[1]

6-2
"SUBJECTS" IN GERUND PHRASES

In gerund phrases, as well as in the grammatical structures taken up in the following chapters, original subjects and objects in full sentences are often changed in form. Thus the full sentence **The hunter shot the birds** becomes the gerund phrase **the hunter's shooting of the birds.** A form like **the hunter's,** which represents the original subject, will be referred to in this and following chapters as the "*subject*"; a form like **of the birds,** which represents the original object, will be referred to as the "*object.*"

A gerund phrase may be used without its "subject" included in the phrase, or it may contain a "subject" in inflected *'s* form or in prepositional form.

A. No "Subject" Included in the Gerund Phrase

The agent for such a gerund phrase may be:

1. Understood as a person in general (**anyone, a person, people,** etc.)—**Playing with guns is dangerous.**

___
[1]In this sentence only the perfect form can indicate past time.

2. Understood from the general context—**He suggested eating dinner at the airport.**
3. Provided in another part of the sentence—**On seeing the damage he had done, the child felt ashamed.** (The agent of **seeing** is **child**, the *subject* of the main verb.); **We thanked them for making such a generous contribution.** (The agent of **making** is **them**, the *object* of the main verb.)

Make a "subjectless" gerund phrase out of the words in parentheses. Make whatever changes or additions are necessary. Note where either the general or the perfect forms may be used.

EXAMPLE: a. (fish, this lake) is forbidden.
          Fishing in this lake is forbidden.

         b. Our people insist on (represent, in, government).
          Our people insist on being represented in the government.

1. He doesn't enjoy (drive, night).

_____

2. (bring up, that subject) will only cause trouble.

_____

3. Some household chores are (make, beds) and (wash, dishes).

_____

4. (criticize, by anyone) hurts his feelings.

_____

5. A law once prohibited Americans from (make, or, buy, liquor).

_____

6. The city official denied (do, anything, improper).

_____

7. I look forward to (see, you, next week).

_____

8. She scolded the cook for (not, put, enough salt, soup).

_____

9. He suggested (take, long walk, early, morning).

_____

10. (Fly, in, airplane) can now be almost as comfortable as (sit, in, living room).

_____

11. We appreciated (be, able, see, you, again.)

_____

12. Please refrain from (talk, driver, while, bus, be, in motion).

_____

13. (Tip, the waiters, ten to fifteen percent) is the custom here.

_____

14. She finished (iron, clothes, few minutes ago).

_____

15. Did you enjoy (visit, White House)?

_____

B. "Subject" in Inflected Possessive Form

> The girl resents *her sister's* getting more attention than she does.
>
> The idea of *Harold's* getting a job as a traveling salesman doesn't appeal to his wife.

Informal usage, however, sometimes permits the unchanged form of a noun, or the object form of a personal pronoun in a gerund phrase after a verb or a preposition.

> We can't understand **them** doing a thing like that.
>
> I don't approve of a **woman** walking by herself at night.

If the "subject" represents a thing, or an idea, the unchanged form of a noun is generally preferred—**Instead of *her health* improving after the operation, it got worse.**

Make a gerund phrase out of the words in parentheses, using the inflected possessive form for the "subject" of the gerund.

EXAMPLE: a. The doctor recommended (we, move, drier climate).

         The doctor recommended our moving to a drier climate.

         b. (the general, slap, wounded soldier) caused quite a scandal.

         The general's slapping a wounded soldier caused quite a scandal.

1. (they, break off, negotiations, so soon) was quite unexpected.

_____

2. (he, return, reward money) surprised the donor.

_____

3. I can't understand (they, reject, advice, their lawyer).

_____

4. No one was aware of his presence because of (he, enter, room, so quietly).

_____

5. The doctor suggested (he, see, psychiatrist).

_____

6. I detest (he, boast, his children).

_____

7. I can't imagine (he, do, anything wrong).

_____

8. He has always resented (his father, tell him, what to do).

_____

C. "Subject" an OF Phrase

A gerund phrase with an **of** phrase "subject" is usually introduced by **the.** Such an **of** phrase "subject" occurs mostly with intransitive verbs—**The shouting of the children disturbed his sleep.**

If the subject represents a live being, it may be put in either an **of** phrase or in *'s* possessive form—**the shouting of the children** or **the children's shouting.** (However, only the inflected form is used if the "subject" is a personal pronoun—*Their* **shouting disturbed his sleep**); and only the **of** phrase is used if the "subject" is long—**The shouting** *of the men in the tavern* **disturbed his sleep.**

Make a gerund phrase out of the words in parentheses, using an **of** phrase for the "subject." Put the **of** phrase immediately after the gerund. Note where the **'s** possessive form may also be used.

EXAMPLE: a. He was awakened by (the dog, bark).

        He was awakened by the barking of the dog.

        (*also* He was awakened by the dog's barking.)

      b. (the pipes, burst) was caused by the extreme cold.

        The bursting of the pipes was caused by the extreme cold.

1. She was deeply touched by (the wounded men, suffer).

_____

2. All American pupils learn about (Pilgrims, land, at, Plymouth Rock, 1620).

_____

3. (lake, freeze over) occurred earlier than usual this year.

_____

4. (leaves, rustle, in, wind) was like music to him.

_____

5. (her daughters, cough, night) disturbed her sleep.

_____

6. (a bomb, explode, their front lawn) frightened them.

_____

7. The political candidate was gratified by (the crowd, cheer).

_____

8. (the people, gamble, at, casino) was repulsive to the old lady.

_____

9. Some newspapers failed to report (the prisoners, riot).

_____

6-3

THE + GERUND + *OF* PHRASE "OBJECT"

If **the** precedes the gerund, the "object" is contained within an **of** phrase.

> **The** storing **of** the merchandise became a problem after the warehouse burned down.[2]
>
> *but* Storing the merchandise became a problem after the warehouse burned down.

Usually the phrase beginning with **the** has stronger noun force. In some gerund phrases, the choice with the **of** phrase "object" is avoided—**Taking drugs is detrimental to the health.**

Make a gerund phrase out of the words in parentheses, using an **of** phrase "object." Note where it is also possible or desirable to use an "object" without **of**.

EXAMPLE: a. The school administration is opposed to (shorten, school year).

The school administration is opposed to the shortening of the school year.

also The School administration is opposed to shortening the school year.

        b. (bribe, officials) is a very serious offense.

The bribing of officials is a very serious offense.

also Bribing officials is a very serious offense.

1. The office boy is responsible for (mail, packages).

_____

2. (light, torches, night) is a beautiful ceremony in Hawaii.

_____

[2]Sometimes another determiner than **the** may be used with an **of** phrase object— **Their** (*or* **this, any**) storing of the merchandise became a problem after the warehouse burned down.

3. The world was shocked to hear about (loot and burn, besieged town).

_____

4. (place, wreaths, servicemen's graves) takes place on Memorial Day.

_____

5. The little girl was puzzled by (come and go, so many people).

_____

6. (burn, trash, outdoors) should be done in a safe place.

_____

7. (build, moderately-priced houses) has stopped for a while.

_____

8. There are mechanical devices for (open and close, these doors).

_____

9. Newspapers are responsible for (shaping, public opinion).

_____

6-4
GERUND PHRASE OBJECTS OF VERBS

Certain verbs are followed by gerund phrase objects. The most common of these verbs are:

acknowledge	deny	miss
admit	enjoy	postpone
advise	finish	practice
anticipate	give up (= stop)	put off
appreciate	justify	recommend
avoid	keep on	resent
cannot help	mention	resist
consider	mind (in questions and negatives)	risk
delay	understand	stop
suggest		

The perfect gerund is often used after these verbs to emphasize time that precedes that of the main verb.

Make gerund phrases out of the words in parentheses. Note where perfect gerunds may also be used.

EXAMPLE: a. I enjoy (play piano).

I enjoy playing the piano. (**I** is the "subject" of the gerund)

   b. We appreciate (you, help, our friends, last night).

We appreciate your helping (*or* having helped) our friends last night.

(**You** is the "subject" of the gerund)

1. I anticipated (have, some trouble, with them).

_____

2. He admitted (steal, the car).

_____

3. She always avoids (talk, that subject).

_____

4. He denied (act, improperly, the matter).

_____

5. The child enjoys (listen, fairy tales).

_____

6. They finished (paint, house) yesterday.

_____

7. The government is trying to justify (increase, income taxes).

_____

8. You must practice (play, piano) if you want to be good at it.

_____

9. I recommend (you, study, report, very carefully).

_____

10. He bitterly resented (dismissed, without any reason).

_____

11. After their quarrel, they stopped (talk, each other).

_____

12. I can understand (you, want, vacation, now).

_____

13. We can't help (feel, sorry, him).

_____

14. The patient risks (lose, eyesight, altogether) if the operation on his eyes is not successful.

_____

_____

15. We appreciate (he, tell, us, truth).

_____

_____

GERUND PHRASE OBJECTS OF PREPOSITIONS

Gerund phrases may function as prepositional objects (*They spoke about having a house-warming party soon*) or as objects in adverbial prepositional phrases (*After listening to the news, she started to prepare dinner*).

A. Gerund Phrases as Prepositional Objects

Supply the required preposition and the gerund form of the verb in parentheses.

EXAMPLE: a. He was accused (kill) <u>of killing</u> his neighbor.

b. I disapprove (he, do) <u>of his doing</u> business that way.

1. I am looking forward (see) _____

_____ you again.[3]

2. Can I plan[4] (see) _____ _____ the new house soon?

3. Nothing will deter him (continue) _____

_____ his experiment.

4. He pleaded guilty (attack) _____

_____ the man.

5. The doctor warned him (take) _____

_____ too many sleeping pills.

6. She reproached her husband (never take) _____

_____ _____ her out at night.

7. Our secretary sometimes complains (not have) _____

_____ enough work to do.

8. We are opposed (they receive) _____

_____ _____ the contract for the building.

9. The couple argued (he, take) _____

_____ his secretary to lunch so often.

[3]**To** is a preposition after the verbs **look forward, object, plead guilty,** as well as after the participial adjectives **used, accustomed, opposed.**
[4]**Plan** may also be followed by the infinitive—**plan to see.**

10. Would you object (I, go) _____

_____ _____ away for a few days?

11. We count (be given) _____ _____
the same rights as the others.

12. The bad weather prevented them (continue) _____

_____ with the construction.

13. No one can blame you (not want) _____

_____ to go through such an experience again.

14. He was suspected (falsify) _____

_____ the records.

15. He insisted (pay) _____ _____ the

entire bill, although we protested (he, do) _____

_____ this.

16. The success of the experiment depends (we, control) _____ _____

_____ the conditions carefully.

B. Gerund Phrase Objects in Adverbial Prepositional Phrases

Make gerund phrases out of the words in parentheses.

EXAMPLE: a. On (hear, bad news), she began to weep uncontrollably.
On hearing the bad news, she began to weep uncontrollably.

           b. We will begin the service by (say, special prayer).
We will begin the service by saying a special prayer.

1. You must cover the pan before (put, it, oven).

_____

2. Soon after (hit, speeding car) the injured man was taken to the hospital.

_____

3. Because of (he, fail, to pay, his taxes) he was given a prison term.

_____

4. The thief crept into the house without (see, by anyone).

_____

5. He was given a ticket for (drive, without license).

_____

6. The bright young boy advanced quickly from (clean, the shop) to (manage, it).

_____

7. The members voted in favor of (maintain, status quo).

_____

8. In the event of (he, fail, to show up), we have a substitute speaker ready.

_____

9. For the sake of (keep, peace, in, family), she never contradicts her husband.

_____

_____

10. Far from (deny, charge), he admitted very proudly that it was he who had blown up the bridge.

_____

_____

6-6
ADJECTIVES-FROM-ADVERBS
IN GERUND PHRASES

An adverb may remain unchanged when used in initial or final position in a gerund phrase.

His wife was shocked at his **recklessly** breaking the law.
His wife was shocked at his breaking the law **recklessly.**

Often, however, adverbs are transformed to adjectives that precede the gerund.

His wife was shocked at his **reckless** breaking of the law.

This adjective form is required in the **the** + gerund + **of** phrase construction—*The constant dripping of* the water irritated her.

In each set of sentences, replace **this** with a gerund phrase made from the *first sentence.* Change the adverb in the *first* sentence to an adjective preceding the gerund.

EXAMPLE: a. He handled the affair discreetly.
The company appreciated *this*.
The company appreciated his discreet handling of the affair.

b. The hotel was closed unexpectedly.
This left the tourists with no place to stay.
The unexpected closing of the hotel left the tourists with no place to stay.

1. Her mother constantly meddled in her affairs.
This was a source of great annoyance to her.

_____

_____

2. He coughed violently.
   This kept him awake all night.

   _____

3. These figures are being checked carefully.
   This will take a long time.

   _____

4. He stole cars senselessly.
   His parents couldn't understand *this*.

   _____

5. All the prisoners were ruthlessly killed.
   He was shocked at *this*.

   _____

6. The waves crashed loudly against the rocks.
   This prevented him from concentrating on his work.

   _____

   _____

7. The couple next door quarreled continuously.
   They complained about *this*.

   _____

8. He drank and gambled excessively.
   His wife divorced him because of *this*.

   _____

9. The animals in the zoo roared fiercely.
   This frightened the young child.

   _____

10. He stabbed his friend fatally.
    He was arrested for *this*.

    _____

11. They disbanded the army completely.
    This marked the end of the war.

    _____

REVIEW OF GERUND PHRASES

Replace **this** with a gerund phrase made from the *first sentence.*

Gerund Phrases as Subjects

1. *I asked the boss for a raise.*
   This didn't do any good.

   _____

2. *She watered the plants every day.*
   This made them grow faster.

   _____

3. *He looked at me suspiciously.*
   This made me feel uncomfortable.

   _____

4. *The thief returned the money.*
   This surprised everyone.

   _____

5. *The boy drives recklessly.*
   This can cause an accident.

   _____

Gerund Phrases as Objects of Verbs

6. *I asked the boss for a raise.*
   The boss didn't like *this*.

   _____

7. *She watered the plants every day.*
   I appreciated *this*.

   _____

8. *He looked at me suspiciously.*
   I couldn't understand *this*.

   _____

9. *The thief returned the money.*
   The thief admitted *this*.

   _____

10. *The boy drives recklessly.*
    The boy's parents mentioned *this*.

    _____

Gerund Phrases as Objects of Prepositions

11. *I asked the boss for a raise.*
    My colleagues laughed at me for *this*.

    _____

12. *She watered the plants every day.*
    Her father praised her for *this*.

    _____

13. *He looked at me suspiciously.*
    I was annoyed at *this*.

    _____

14. *The thief returned the money.*
    We all remarked about *this*.

    _____

15. *The boy drives recklessly.*
    The boy's parents are concerned about *this*.

    _____

7

Infinitive Phrases

Infinitive phrases may function as nouns, adjectives, or adverbs.

1. *Nominal function*	
a. subject	**For her to clean the house every day** is absolutely necessary.
	or
	It is absolutely necessary **for her to clean the house every day.**
b. object of verb	Her husband wants **her to clean the house every day.**
c. subjective complement (predicate noun)	The regulation is **for boys and girls to live in separate dormitories.**
d. appositive	He had only one desire—**for his family to be in good health.**
2. *Adjectival function*	Here is a letter **for you to type.**
3. *Adverbial function*	
a. modifier of a sentence	**To tell the truth,** I don't understand him at all.
b. modifier of a verb	**(In order) for me to buy a car,** I'll have to take a loan from the bank.
c. modifier of an adjective	I'm sorry **to see you leave.**
	This music is too hard **for me to play correctly.**

7-1
FORMS OF INFINITIVES

	Active Voice	Progressive	Passive Voice
General form (timeless) (present infinitive)	**to offer**	**to be offering**	**to be offered**
Perfect form (past time)	**to have offered**	**to have been offering**	**to have been offered**

Note that all forms of the infinitive begin with **to.** Infinitives are generally made negative by placing **not** before the **to.**

A. General Forms
TO OFFER, TO BE OFFERING,
TO BE OFFERED

These forms express time that is simultaneous with, or future from, that of the main verb.

Supply the required form of the infinitive.

EXAMPLE: a. They expect (see) their new grandson soon.
They expect <u>to see</u> their new grandson soon.

b. They appear (have) an argument.
They appear <u>to be having</u> an argument.

c. He gave the report to his secretary (type).
He gave the report to his secretary <u>to be typed</u>.

1. The children quarreled over who was (get) ＿＿＿＿＿＿ the candy.

2. I don't know how (do) ＿＿＿＿＿＿ this exercise.

3. (understand) ＿＿＿＿＿＿ is (forgive) ＿＿＿＿＿＿.

4. At the present time, he is believed (recuperate) ＿＿＿＿＿＿ from a serious illness.

5. Please give me a vase (put) ＿＿＿＿＿＿ the flowers in.

6. In order (gain) ＿＿＿＿＿＿ the child's confidence, you must be strict but fair with her.

7. In all athletic contests, it is important (not lose) ＿＿＿＿＿＿ sight of the opponent.

8. The child needs (reassure) ＿＿＿＿＿＿ that he is loved.

9. He was happy (relieve) ＿＿＿＿＿＿ of some of his duties.

10. I expect (see) ＿＿＿＿＿＿ him soon.

11. No one is compelling him (work) ＿＿＿＿＿＿ so hard.

12. He appears (have) ＿＿＿＿＿＿ a hard time convincing his employer that he is right.

13. The speaker refused (intimidate) ＿＿＿＿＿＿ by some threats from the audience.

14. The kidnaper forced his victim (get) ＿＿＿＿＿＿ into the car.

15. She asked her daughter (not stay out) ＿＿＿＿＿＿ late at night.

16. This music is (play) ＿＿＿＿＿＿ with great animation.

17. The children appear (enjoy) ＿＿＿＿＿＿ themselves at the party.

B. Perfect Forms
TO HAVE OFFERED, TO HAVE BEEN OFFERING,
TO HAVE BEEN OFFERED

These forms emphasize time that is completed before the time of the main verb. If such emphasis is not desired, the general forms are sometimes also possible.

Supply the perfect infinitive form.

EXAMPLE: a.   I seem (lose) my key.
I seem <u>to have lost</u> my key.

b.   The boy was too young (expose) to such a dangerous situation.
The boy was too young <u>to have been exposed</u> to such a dangerous situation.

1.   I would have given my life (save) _____ hers.

2.   He was found (misappropriate) _____ the funds.

3.   We believe there (be) _____ an accident at the corner a short while ago.

4.   He appeared (circulate, *progressive*) _____ many lies about the company he was working for.

5.   I would like (see) _____ your wife's face when you gave her the diamond ring for her birthday.

6.   He is said (be) _____ unscrupulous in his business dealings in his youth.

7.   He seems (not understand) _____ the instructions that were given him.

8.   The accused man said that it was impossible for him (be) _____ at the scene of the crime because he was in another town.

9.   He was shrewd enough (not deceive) _____ by the promises made at the meeting last night.

7-2
FOR "SUBJECTS"
OF INFINITIVE PHRASES

Many infinitive phrases do not have a "subject" included within them. If the "subject" is contained within the phrase, it may take a prepositional form that precedes the infinitive. The most usual preposition in such a use is **for**.

Make an infinitive phrase out of the words in parentheses. Use a **for** phrase "subject" of the infinitive.

EXAMPLE: a.   It is not easy (I, get up, early).
It is not easy for me to get up early.

b.   (She, swim, English Channel) took a lot of courage.
For her to swim the English Channel took a lot of courage.

1. In order (the children, not get, too tired) they all went to bed early every night during their trip.

_____

_____

2. Her teacher is anxious (the girl, make up, work, she missed, during her illness).

_____

_____

3. It will be necessary (we, get, our passports, this week).

_____

4. The question is too difficult (the students, answer).

_____

5. What I would like is (you, give, I, objective opinion, this matter).

_____

6. It is not possible (anyone, visit, the patient, now).

_____

7. There is too much work (they, take, coffee break).

_____

8. It is useless (we, complain, our neighbor, their loud music).

_____

9. The house is unfit (anyone, live in).

_____

10. He doesn't make enough money (his family, take, vacation, summer.)

_____

7-3
ANTICIPATORY *IT*
WITH INFINITIVE PHRASE SUBJECTS

Infinitive phrase subjects occur chiefly with the verb **be,** causative verbs, verbs of emotion, and a few other verbs like **require, take, mean.**

> For him to get the money now is impossible.
> To dress that way requires courage.

Such infinitive phrase subjects appear more commonly after anticipatory **it.**

> It is impossible for him to get the money now.
> It requires courage to dress that way.

Change the following sentences so that the infinitive subjects are used after anticipatory **it**.

EXAMPLE: For them to lose their only son was a great tragedy.
It was a great tragedy for them to lose their only son.

1. For him to open up his own restaurant business would require a great deal of money.

    _____

2. To be seen in public without a coat and tie would embarrass him.

    _____

3. Not to have a college education is a disadvantage.

    _____

4. To pursue this train of thought would be worthwhile.

    _____

5. Never to see him again would make her very sad.

    _____

6. To keep looking young forever is an ideal of many women.

    _____

7. To cook tasty but economical meals requires much ingenuity.

    _____

8. To get him to come with us won't be easy.

    _____

9. To watch our neighbor's cat come begging for food is amusing.

    _____

10. To change the rebellion into a revolution won't take much.

    _____

11. To hire an inexperienced person is against our policy.

    _____

12. For me to speak in public is very embarrassing.

    _____

13. For us to appeal to him for money would be useless.

    _____

14. To be interrupted while he is writing annoys him very much.

    _____

After anticipatory **it,** the preposition used with the "subject" of the infinitive may be not only **for,** but **of** or **to.**

Of "subjects" *of infinitives after certain adjectives:*

1. **foolish, impertinent, polite, proper, rude, stupid, wicked, wise, wrong** (less commonly, also with **for**);
2. **considerate, generous, good, intelligent, kind, unworthy.**

To "subjects" *of infinitives after* **-ing** *participial adjectives expressing emotional states*— **alarming, amazing, amusing, disappointing, embarrassing, irritating, shocking,** etc. (With some of these adjectives, **for** is also occasionally used.)

Of or *to* "subjects" unlike **for** "subjects," must remain after the predicate adjectives.

A. Make infinitive phrases from the words in parentheses. Use **of** or **to** before the "subject" of the infinitive. Note where **for** may also be used.

EXAMPLE: a. It would be foolish (you, stop, now).

It would be foolish of you (*less commonly* for you) to stop now.

b. It was amazing (I, learn, how young, mayor, be).

It was amazing to me to learn how young the mayor was.

1. It was very impertinent (the child, make, such, remark).

_____

2. It was rude (that man, not, to take, hat, off, in, elevator).

_____

3. It's wrong (they, give, the child, everything, he, want).

_____

4. It is distressing (we, see, how thin and pale, she, become).

_____

5. It was embarrassing (he, be, so highly praised).

_____

6. It was shocking (the audience, see, so much, violence, on, screen).

_____

7. It was generous (you, give, all, that money, blind man).

_____

8. It is fascinating (the child, observe, way, toy, work).

_____

9. It is unworthy (public official, accept, bribe).

_____

10. It is satisfying (her parents, know, that, her husband, be, very kind, she).

_____

11. It was kind (you, visit, I, in, hospital).

_____

12. It is irritating (I, hear, she, always, complaining).

_____

13. It was not polite (young child, take, last piece, cake).

_____

B. Some sentences containing adjectives followed by **of** phrases may be expressed in another way.

It was foolish **of you** to do that.
or
You were foolish to do that.

Use the adjectives in the first column to write two alternate sentences with the infinitive.

EXAMPLE: impertinent   The child hit his mother.
It was impertinent of the child to hit his mother.
The child was impertinent to hit his mother.

1. considerate   You visited me in the hospital.

_____

_____

2. unwise   You went to work with a very bad cold.

_____

_____

3. wrong   You are condemning them without knowing the facts.

_____

_____

4. impolite   They left their neighbor's party right after dinner was over.

_____

_____

5. foolish   He put all his savings in such a risky business.

_____

_____

6. wise   You didn't follow his bad advice.

_____

_____

7. stupid   They think they can change such a serious situation overnight.

_____

_____

8. kind   You concern yourself with my problems.

_____

_____

9. wicked   The children tease the little boy so much.

_____

_____

C. Some sentences with adjectives followed by **to** phrases may be expressed in two other ways.

It was shocking **to me** to hear the news of his death.
or
It shocked me to hear the news of his death.
or
I was shocked to hear the news of his death.

Combine each set of sentences in the three ways shown in the example.

EXAMPLE: This amazed me.
      I saw how tall the boy had grown.

      It was amazing to me to see how tall the boy had grown.

      It amazed me to see how tall the boy had grown.

      I was amazed to see how tall the boy had grown.

1. This discouraged me.
  We learned that our rent was going to be raised.

_____

_____

2. This embarrassed the speaker.
   He realized that his audience was not paying attention to his lecture.

   _____

   _____

   _____

3. This startled me.
   I heard a strange noise coming from the other room.

   _____

   _____

   _____

4. This surprised me.
   I saw how strong this fragile-looking woman really was.

   _____

   _____

   _____

5. This embarrassed him.
   He was praised for winning first prize.

   _____

   _____

   _____

6. This disappointed him.
   He didn't get the promotion he was expecting.

   _____

   _____

   _____

7. This annoyed the entertainer.
   He heard some people talking during his performance.

   _____

   _____

   _____

8. This satisfied them.
   They were remembered in their uncle's will.

   _____

   _____

   _____

INFINITIVE PHRASES AS OBJECTS OF VERBS

Verbs taking infinitive objects may be divided into three groups according to what functions as the "subject" of the infinitive.

1. *The **subject** of the main verb is the "subject" of the infinitive*

afford	endeavor	refuse
arrange	fail	resolve
bother	forget	seek
care (*neg. and*	happen	seem
interrog.)	hope	strive
choose (= prefer)	learn	struggle
claim	manage	swear
consent	mean	tend
decide	offer	threaten
demand	pretend	undertake
deserve	promise	venture
determine	proceed	volunteer

I can't afford to buy a new coat.
(The infinitive **to buy** refers to **I**, the *subject* of the main verb **can't afford.**)

2. *The **object** of the main verb is the "subject" of the infinitive*

advise	empower	motivate
allow	enable	oblige
cause	encourage	order
caution	entitle	permit
challenge	forbid	persuade
coerce	force	remind
command	get (= cause)	request
compel	implore	require
condemn	incite	send
convince	induce	teach
dare (= challenge)	instruct	tell
defy	invite	tempt
direct		urge

I advised you to buy a new coat.
(The infinitive **to buy** refers to **you**, the *object* of the main verb **advised.**)
Sentences with these infinitives can be made passive.

You were advised to buy a new coat.

3. *Either the* **subject** *or the* **object** *of the main verb may be the "subject" of the infinitive*

ask	expect	prefer
beg	like	want
desire	love	wish

I want to buy a new coat.

(**To buy** refers to **I,** the *subject* of **want.**)

I want you to buy a new coat.

(**To buy** refers to **you,** the *object* of **want.**)

Form an infinitive phrase from the words in parentheses.

Infinitives Referring to Subjects of Main Verbs

EXAMPLE: a. We expect (receive, his letter, few weeks).

   We expect to receive his letter in a few weeks. (**to receive** refers to the subject **we**)

   b. He deserves (punish, what he did).

   He deserves to be punished for what he did. (**to be punished** refers to the subject **he**)

1.   He failed (appear, court, when, he, suppose to).

_____

2.   We hope (improve, this machine, near future).

_____

3.   They are planning (cross, ocean).

_____

4.   Would you care (have, your car, wash)?

_____

5.   He claims (descend, a royal family).

_____

6.   They were resolved (carry through, plan, they, make).

_____

7.   He always manages (assign, easiest tasks).

_____

8.   She desires (not, disturb, an hour).

_____

9. The boy is pretending (be, son, millionaire).

_____

10. The accused man has refused (intimidate, police).

_____

11. He swore (never, see, her, again).

_____

12. The couple decided (not, go, that restaurant, again).

_____

13. The police are endeavoring (locate, the parents, lost child).

_____

14. They are preparing (go, Africa).

_____

15. I hope you will learn (be, patient, with, children, your class).

_____

Infinitives Referring to Objects of Main Verbs

EXAMPLE: a. The doctor advised her (get, more rest).

The doctor advised her to get more rest (**active** main verb—**to get** refers to the object **her**)

b. She was advised (get, more rest).

She was advised to get more rest. (**passive** main verb—**to get** refers to an original object)

1. He has defied his landlord (evict, he, his home).

_____

2. The accident caused the victim (lose, eyesight).

_____

3. This coupon will entitle you (receive, 10% discount).

_____

4. She implored her husband (not, leave, she).

_____

5. He was invited (lecture, subject, ecology).

_____

6. He was finally permitted (leave, country).

_____

7. In the old days a man could be challenged (fight, duel, pistols or swords).

_____

8. Please remind me (take, my pill, lunchtime).

_____

9. The students have been forbidden (smoke, the classroom).

_____

10. The plumber asked them (turn off, water, few minutes).

_____

11. His parents warned him (not, come, home, so late).

_____

12. All new students are required (report, health office, soon, possible).

_____

13. He was warned (not, tell, what, he, know).

_____

7-6
INFINITIVE vs. GERUND SUBJECTS

The greatest choice between the infinitive and the gerund is as subject. The infinitive generally represents an act or state as a whole, whereas the gerund represents an act or state in progress. *This kind of choice occurs more often if the main verb is* **present or future.**

To learn (*or* learning) a new language is difficult.
For us to back out (*or* our backing out) of the agreement would create much resentment.

Where possible, replace the verb in parentheses with *both a gerund and an infinitive* and make whatever change is needed. Keep in mind that the infinitive is more restricted in its use as a subject than the gerund is.

EXAMPLE: a. (We, locate) a suitable place for a meeting will take some time.
      For us to locate (*or* Our locating) a suitable place for a meeting will take some time.

      b. (Interrogate) by the police is quite an ordeal.
      To be interrogated (*or* Being interrogated) by the police is quite an ordeal.

      c. (He, put) on parole was recommended by the prison authorities.
      His being put on parole was recommended by the prison authorities.
      (The infinitive is generally not used with a past verb or a passive main verb.)

1. (the committee, investigate) the matter now would only cause the government embarrassment.

   _____

2. (Live) at home would save that student a lot of money.

   _____

3. (Inherit) money one doesn't expect is a pleasant surprise.

   _____

4. (He, insult) the officer resulted in his arrest.

   _____

5. (The children, take) so long to dress always annoyed their mother.

   _____

6. (Entertain) the troops is the only thing the singer does now.

   _____

7. (Plant) a garden takes skill and patience.

   _____

8. (Save face) is more important in some cultures than in others.

   _____

9. (Type) that long report will be expensive.

   _____

10. (Rebuild) the cathedral that was bombed will cost a great deal of money.

    _____

11. (Ship) the goods will take over a month.

    _____

12. (Overlook) our own faults is easy to do.

    _____

13. (He, do) that requires a lot of courage.

    _____

7-7
INFINITIVE vs. GERUND OBJECTS

Some verbs may be followed by either infinitive phrase objects or gerund phrase objects.

attempt	hesitate	regret
cannot bear (*also*	intend	remember
interrog.)	like	cannot stand (*also*
begin	love	*interrog.*)
commence	neglect	start
continue	plan	try
hate		

After **regret, remember,** the gerund often refers to past time, the infinitive to future time.

I remember taking care (*or* having taken care) of that matter. (past time)
I must remember to take care of that matter. (future time)

Use the infinitive or gerund form of the verb. If either form of verbal object may be used, give both.

EXAMPLE: a. They will begin (harvest) the wheat today.
They will begin to harvest (*or* harvesting) the wheat today. (The infinitive or the gerund may be used after **begin.**)

b. We missed (see) you at the meeting.
We missed seeing you at the meeting. (Only the gerund object is used after **miss.**)

c. We arranged (meet) him at the station.
We arranged to meet him at the station. (Only the infinitive is used after **arrange.**)

1. The farmers risk (lose) their crops if it doesn't rain soon.

_____

2. We enjoyed (meet) you last night.

_____

3. They will continue (work) seven days a week until the building is finished.

_____

4. I expect (finish) the work next week.

_____

5. We must never neglect (do) our duty.

_____

6. He started (have) trouble with his skin a year ago.

_____

7. I like (get up) early.

_____

8. Try (go) to bed earlier.[1]

_____

9. The boy refused (do) what he was told.

_____

10. The cashier admitted (take) the money from the cash register.

_____

11. She stopped (visit) her brother after a bitter quarrel they had.[2]

_____

12. She can never resist (contradict) her husband.

_____

13. We regret (advise) you that we no longer manufacture the item you have ordered.

_____

14. They finished (take) inventory a few days ago.

_____

15. The driver put on his brakes to avoid (hit) the car in front of him.

_____

16. I forgot (mail) the letter my wife gave me yesterday.[3]

_____

17. I must remember (mail) these letters.

_____

[1]**Try** + the infinitive usually means "make a greater effort," while **try** + the gerund means "perform as a kind of experiment." In this sentence either meaning is appropriate.

[2]The gerund object is used after **stop,** unless an adverbial of purpose is intended— **We stopped at a service station to get some gas.** (purpose)

[3]Sometimes the gerund object is used after **forget,** especially with a negative or interrogative verb—**Who can ever forget winning a million dollars in the lottery?**

7-8
TO-LESS INFINITIVES
OR *-ING* PARTICIPLES IN TWO-PART OBJECTS

Some verbs are followed by two-part objects containing **to**-less infinitives as the second part.

1. The causative verbs **make** (= compel), **have**

    She made the children clean up their own rooms.
    She had the maid clean all the rooms.[4]

2. **Let** (= *allow*), **bid** (= *request*)

    They let the children stay up late on weekends.
    She bid the children be quiet.

3. **Help** (the omission of **to** is optional)

    He helped the old woman (to) cross the street.

4. Verbs of perception (**feel, hear, listen to, look at, notice, observe, overhear, see, watch, witness**) as an alternative for the participial form.

    I heard the whistle blow (or blowing) a few minutes ago.
    She watched the passengers get (or getting) off the bus.

When the passive of such verbs is used, the **to** is usually required.

    The children were made to clean their own rooms.
    She was helped to see the error of her ways.
    He was heard to say that he would get revenge.

A. To-less Infinitives

Use infinitive phrases in a two-part object based on the words in parentheses. Only passive main verbs will require the use of **to** before the infinitive.

EXAMPLE: a. Her absence made (he, realize, how much, he, love, she).
    Her absence made him realize how much he loved her.

b. The musician was made (understand, he, can, not practice, late, night).
    The musician was made to understand (that) he could not practice late at night.

1. The teacher is planning to have (all, children, write, story).

    _____

2. The city officials made (old lady, get rid, some, her cats).

    _____

---

[4]See Exer. 5-7 for the alternate way to express this sentence with the past participle—**She had all the rooms cleaned.**

3.   Their parents let (children, stay up, late, Saturday night).

_____

4.   She felt (blood, run, down, cheek).

_____

5.   He was helped (understand, he can, not, have, his own way, all, time).

_____

6.   Plese let (I, carry, those packages, you).

_____

7.   She bid (her husband, be, careful, when, he, return, home, late, night).

_____

8.   He was listening (a bird, sing, outside, his window).

_____

9.   Can you help (I, locate, Main Street, this map)?

_____

10. We heard (clock, strike, one).

_____

11. The teacher made (all, poor students, take, test, again).

_____

12. He is helping (his neighbors, paint, their house).

_____

13. I had (auto mechanic, change, tire, my car).

_____

14. We noticed (woman, come out, house).

_____

15. The club made (new members, undergo, an initiation).

_____

16. We had (carpenter, build, large cabinet).

_____

B. To-less Infinitives or Participles After Verbs of Perception

After the verbs of perception, either a **to-less** infinitive or a participle may be used—**She watched the children** *cross* (*or crossing*) **the street.** The participle emphasizes the duration of an action.

Form two-part objects from the words in parentheses. In some of these objects, the infinitive will be preferred, in others, the participle; in still others, either one may be used.

EXAMPLE: a.   He felt (something, go wrong, motor, his car).
He felt something go wrong with the motor of his car.

b.   We heard (some people, sing, in, street).
We heard some people singing in the street.

c.   He listened (orchestra, rehearse, next performance).
He listened to the orchestra rehearsing (*or* rehearse) for the next performance.

1.   Can't you feel (that ant, crawl, your face)?

_____

2.   I heard (their car, pass, by, here, few minutes ago).

_____

3.   He listened reverently (minister, deliver, sermon, brotherly love).

_____

4.   Just look (she, pretend, not, notice, we).

_____

5.   The teacher noticed (one, the children, draw, beautiful picture).

_____

6.   The child was last seen (talk, some schoolmates, schoolyard).

_____

7.   I overheard (they, gossip, our neighbors).

_____

8.   We observed (storekeeper, close, store, early, that day).

_____

9.   They were heard (say, they, never, come back, that restaurant, in, future).

_____

10.   After we drove for several miles, we saw (some mountains, loom, the distance).

_____

11.   She felt (the tears, come, her eyes).

_____

12.   Suddenly the air raid sirens were heard (warn, people, take shelter).

_____

INFINITIVE PHRASES
AS ALTERNATIVES FOR ADJECTIVE CLAUSES

In infinitive-phrase alternatives for adjective clauses, the noun or pronoun being modified usually represents the "subject" or "object" of the infinitive.

> She has no one to help her. (= who can help her)
> **No one** is the "subject" of **help.**

> There are still many things for me to do. (= which I must do)
> **Things** is the "object" of **do.**

> The next question to be considered (= which must be considered) is the crucial one.
> **Question** is the "subject" of the passive **be considered.**

Often an active infinitive alternates with a passive one—*the next question to consider.* The infinitive phrase may also be an alternative for an adjectival **when** clause (**the best time to do it** = when you should do it) or a **where** clause (**a quiet place to study** = where you can study).

Many adjective clauses that may be replaced by infinitive phrases contain modal auxiliaries such as **can, must, should.** The infinitive phrase is often preferred for its greater simplicity.

Change the adjective clauses to infinitive phrases. Note where an active or a passive infinitive may be used.

EXAMPLE: a. On our farm there are many animals which we need to feed.

On our farm there are many animals (for us) to feed. (The **for** phrase "subject" is often omitted if it can be implied from the rest of the sentence.) (*also,* many animals to be fed)

b. The dishes which you have to wash are stacked on the kitchen counter.

The dishes for you to wash are stacked on the kitchen counter. (*also,* the dishes to be washed)

c. The packages which must be taken to the post office are over there.

The packages to be taken to the post office are over there. (*also,* the packages to take to the post office)

1. He was the first guest who arrived at the picnic.

_____

2. Here is the meat which should be put in the refrigerator.

_____

3. There is no more work that we need to do tonight.

_____

4. I have two important phone calls which I must make.

_____

5. The sales manager dictated some letters which had to be typed right away.

_____

_____

6. They will have to hire someone who can guide them through the jungle.

_____

7. The letters which need to be answered immediately are usually put in a special folder.

_____

_____

8. Here are the books which must be returned to the library.

_____

9. The best time when you can see him is in the morning.

_____

10. One of the best places where you can buy good fish is at Fisherman's Wharf.

_____

_____

11. The only time that you can find him at home is in the evening.

_____

12. The worst place where you might build your new home is near the highway.

_____

_____

7-10
INFINITIVE PHRASES
AS ALTERNATIVES FOR ADVERBIAL CLAUSES

Infinitive phrases often represent alternatives for adverbial clauses of purpose, condition, or cause.

Purpose	**He moved his chair to be closer to her.** (infinitive = so that he might be closer to her) **They will have to blast through the mountains (in order) to build the highway.** (*In order to* strengthens the meaning of purpose.)
Condition	**I would have given my life to have saved theirs.** (infinitive = if I could have saved theirs, or in order that I might have saved theirs—condition and purpose are often linked.) **She must have deeply resented his remarks, to judge by her reaction.** (infinitive = if we are to judge by her reaction)

Cause **He rejoiced to see his old friends again.**
(infinitive = because he saw his old friends again)
I was pleased to see him again.
(infinitive = because I saw him again)

As with adverbial clauses, adverbial infinitive phrases that are felt as loosely attached to the main verb (nonrestrictive phrases) may also appear at the beginning of a sentence or clause—**To judge by her reaction, she must have deeply resented his remarks.**

Change the adverbial clauses to infinitive phrases. Note which phrases may appear in more than one position. Use commas after introductory infinitive phrases.

EXAMPLE: a. You must leave early in the morning if you want to get to work by nine o'clock.
You must leave early in the morning (in order) to get to work by nine o'clock.

or To get to work by nine o'clock, you must leave early in the morning.

b. The men must work overtime in order that the building may be finished on time.
The men must work overtime for the building to be finished on time.

or For the building to be finished on time, the men must work overtime.

1. They stopped the car so that they could admire the sunset from the lookout.

_____

_____

2. I would be ashamed if I lived in such a dirty house.

_____

3. He will do anything if he might have the chance to see her again.

_____

4. We will have to mail this package today in order that it can get there on time.

_____

_____

5. He decided to go to school at night so that he might study engineering.

_____

_____

6. So that he might make his lectures more interesting, the lecturer used colored slides.

_____

_____

7. You would be surprised if you learned how much it costs to live in that neighborhood.

_____

_____

8.   We were pleased because we saw how well the work was done.

_____

_____

9.   If our dance is to be successful, we must prepare everything carefully beforehand.

_____

_____

10.   If you want to live in that house, you will have to pay a very high rent.

_____

_____

11.   I'll be satisfied if I can get my money back out of this business deal.

_____

12.   He decided to learn to swim in order that he might overcome his fear of water.

_____

_____

13.   I would be delighted if I could meet your family.

_____

7-11
INFINITIVES PLUS
PREPOSITIONAL PARTICLES

A prepositional particle may be inseparable from an infinitive.

Infinitive phrase used in noun function (as a subject or object):

He expects **to be taken care of.** (The infinitive is passive only.)

Infinitive phrase used as an *adjective* modifying a noun:

This is a good company **to work for.** (active infinitive)
That is a good company **to be associated with.** (passive infinitive)

We have already seen that both the active and the passive infinitive may be possible in an adjectival infinitive phrase.

There still remains much furniture **to dispose of.**
There still remains much furniture **to be disposed of.**

Some of these infinitive adjectivals may have alternate forms which include the relative pronoun—**That is a good company** *for which to work,* or *with which to be associated.*

A. Infinitives Plus
Particles Used as Nominals

Change the infinitive phrases from active to passive. Omit all subjects and objects from the infinitive phrases.

EXAMPLE: a. She doesn't want (anyone to stare at her).
             <u>She doesn't want to be stared at.</u>

                  b. (For anyone to take advantage of us) isn't pleasant.
             <u>To be taken advantage of isn't pleasant.</u>

1.   No one likes (anyone to laugh at him).

_____

2.   (For people to think well of him) has always been important to him.

_____

3.   It disturbs him (for anyone to impose on him).

_____

4.   They don't intend (for anyone to interfere with them).

_____

5.   (For people to look up to him) has been his dream for many years.

_____

6.   He doesn't like (anyone to look down on him).

_____

7.   She didn't expect (the teacher to call on her) in class.

_____

B. Infinitives Plus
Particles Used as Adjectivals

Replace the words in parentheses by an infinitive plus a prepositional particle. Use an active or passive infinitive. (For some sentences both active and passive infinitives are possible.)

EXAMPLE: a. We still have a few more matters (which we must deal with).
             <u>We still have a few more matters to deal with,</u> *or* <u>to be dealt with.</u>

                  b. That is a noble goal (which you should strive for).
             <u>That is a noble goal to strive for.</u>

                  c. Right now he has many problems (which he must cope with).
             <u>Right now he has many problems to cope with.</u>

1. The best person (whom you should talk to) is the factory superintendent.

---

2. He would like to have more tasks (which he can be responsible for).

---

3. Please give me a pan (which I can put my potatoes in).

---

4. I have a few more matters (which I must attend to) before I can leave.

---

5. He needs more money (which he can live on).

---

6. The girl doesn't have many friends (with whom she can play).

---

7. There is no one here (that you need to be afraid of).

---

8. There are still many things (that I must take care of).

7-12
INFINITIVE PHRASES
AFTER *TOO, ENOUGH*

Infinitive phrases may follow adjectives or adverbs used with **too** or **enough**.

too	She's too intelligent **to be deceived by such a lie.** It's raining too hard **for me to go out.**
enough	The canoe is large enough **to hold four people.** We can't get to the theater soon enough **to see the play from the beginning.**

Note that the word **enough** follows the adjective or adverb it modifies.

Combine the following sentences, using too or enough plus an infinitive phrase.

EXAMPLE: a. They're very poor. They can't buy a house.
They're too poor to buy a house.

b. The car is very large. It can seat six people comfortably.
The car is large enough to seat six people comfortably.

c. They're very far ahead. We can't catch up with them.
They're too far ahead for us to catch up with them. (Note that a **for** phrase is used if the "subject" of the infinitive phrase is different from the subject of the sentence.)

1. She has very many students in the class. She can't give them individual attention.

_____

2. He's very stingy. He won't buy his wife a good coat.

_____

3. This piece of material is not very big. I can't make a dress out of it.

_____

4. The roads are very icy. We can't drive on them.

_____

5. Her father has been away a long time. The little girl can't remember him.

_____

6. We have plenty of food. We can serve all the extra guests.

_____

7. I don't have much carbon paper. I can't make five copies.

_____

8. He's worked very hard and long. He won't give up now.

_____

9. She changed very gradually. We didn't notice the deterioration of her health.

_____

10. I have very much homework. I can't go to the movies with you.

_____

11. They can't work very quickly. They can't rescue the injured mountain climbers before dark.

_____

12. The professor spoke very slowly. The foreign students understood him.

_____

7-13
REVIEW OF INFINITIVE PHRASES

Infinitive Phrases as Subjects

Replace the word **this** in one sentence with an *infinitive phrase* made from the *other* sentence in italics. (Where possible, use anticipatory **it** also.)

1. *Come home at once.*
   This is necessary.

_____

2. *He wrote me a nasty letter.*
   This was insulting.

_____

3. *He came here at a busy time.*
   This is inconsiderate.

_____

4. *The African nations can become industrialized.*
   This requires a great deal of work.

_____

_____

Infinitive Phrases as Objects of Verbs

5. *The man was to halt at once.*
   The guard commanded *this*.

_____

6. *She sews very well.*
   Her mother taught her *this*.

_____

7. *Have lunch with me.*
   I would like *this*.

_____

Infinitive Phrases as Subjective Complements

8. The present fad is *this*.
   The young people are wearing sneakers.

_____

9. The plan that Woodrow Wilson suggested was *this*.
   A League of Nations should be set up to help prevent future wars.

_____

_____

Infinitive Phrases Instead of Adjective Clauses

Change the italicized adjective clauses into infinitive phrases.

10. Here are some papers *which you ought to examine*.

_____

11. There are many things *which must be done* before we can leave.

_____

12. Nighttime is the time *when we can relax and watch television*.

_____

13. He is the man *whom you should consult on this matter*.

_____

Infinitive Phrases
Instead of Adverbial Clauses

Change the italicized adverbial clauses into infinitive phrases.

14. I would be ashamed *if I received such low grades*.

_____

15. We are happy *that we can see you again*.

_____

16. We have enough money *so that we can take a long vacation*.

_____

17. He held up the picture *so that everyone could see it*.

_____

8

Absolute Constructions

The term *absolute* refers to a free grammatical element within a sentence. It usually has no connecting word that relates it to the rest of the sentence.

Absolute constructions are also called nominative absolutes because they include a noun "subject."

TYPES OF ABSOLUTE CONSTRUCTIONS

1. *With verb (participle)*
   a. general form
      (1) active — **The train being late,** we missed our plane.
      (2) passive — **Their home ruined by the fire,** they had to ask their neighbors for shelter

   b. perfect form
      (1) active — **The play having ended,** we went backstage to congratulate the actors.
      (2) passive — **Their crops having been destroyed by the floods,** the farmers appealed to the government for help.

2. *Without verb*
   (form of **be** *omitted)*
   Predicate of absolute is:
   a. a noun — **His former palatial home now a summer resort,** he reflected on the sad turn of events which had brought this about.
   b. an adjective — The old mining town was utterly deserted, **its streets gray and dead.**
   c. a prepositional phrase — She looked at the man curiously, **her head slightly to one side.**
   d. an adverb — **His terrible ordeal over,** he did nothing but sleep for several days.

   e. *Preceded by* **with**
   a. with verb — She stood before him hopefully, **with the letter of recommendation held tightly in her hand.**
   b. without verb — She stood before him hopefully, **with the letter of recommendation in her hand.**

ABSOLUTE CONSTRUCTIONS WITH PARTICIPLES

An absolute construction contains a "subject" that is unchanged from the form it has in a full sentence. In the predicate, the verb has participial **-ing** or **-ed** form, or if the verb is **be,** it may be omitted entirely.

This construction usually appears at the beginning or end of a sentence and is set off from the rest of the sentence with a comma. It is made negative by placing **not** before the predicate part.

Combine each set of sentences by changing the italicized sentence to an absolute construction. Keep the absolute construction in the same position as the sentence from which it has been made. Set off the construction with a comma.

General Forms
Offering, Offered,
Being offered

The general forms express the same time as that of the main verb.

EXAMPLE: a. *Tears were streaming down her face.*
The child ran home to be comforted by her mother.

<u>Tears streaming down her face, the child ran home to be comforted by her mother.</u>

b. *Their plot was discovered.*
The conspirators had to flee for their lives.

<u>Their plot (being) discovered, the conspirators had to flee for their lives.</u>

c. The girl walked along gracefully.
The huge basket on her head did not seem to be a heavy burden at all.

<u>The girl walked along gracefully, the huge basket on her head not seeming to be a heavy burden at all.</u>

1. *The men began to pour out from the factory.*
She watched to see which one was her husband.

_____

_____

2. *His health was regained.*
He was happy to return to work.

_____

_____

3. *Their air conditioner was not working properly again.*
They decided to buy a new one.

_____

_____

4. *His eyes were finally open to her hypocrisy.*
   He wondered how he could ever have been deceived by her wiles.

_____

_____

5. *The rain began to make everyone uncomfortable.*
   They decided to continue their dinner indoors.

_____

_____

6. The judge dismissed the charge against the man.
   There was no conclusive evidence that he had committed the felony.

_____

_____

7. *The labor dispute was finally settled.*
   The pilots began to fly the planes again.

_____

_____

8. *His hotel room was not yet ready.*
   He had to wait until the maid finished cleaning it.

_____

_____

9. *The last guest was gone.*
   The exhausted host and hostess went to bed immediately.

_____

_____

10. *His eyes burned from the smog.*
    He felt he could not go out again that day.

_____

_____

11. *The required documents did not arrive on time.*
    They had to postpone the investigation.

_____

_____

Perfect Forms
Having offered, Having been offering,
Having been offered

The perfect forms refer to time completed before that of the main verb. If there is no desire to stress the completion of one time before another, the general forms may also be used.

EXAMPLE: a. *The floods had made the highway impassable.*
All cars were detoured to the side roads.

The floods having made the highway impassable, all cars were detoured to the side roads.

b. *His knife wounds had been treated by the doctor.*
The young man was released from the hospital.

His knife wounds having been treated by the doctor, the young man was released from the hospital.

c. *The guerrillas had been causing disturbances for some time.*
The government sent their armed forces to the area to wipe them out.

The guerrillas having been causing disturbances for some time, the government sent their armed forces to the area to wipe them out.

1. *The interest rate had been lowered.*
More people began to take out loans from the bank.

_____

_____

2. *Her car had stopped suddenly in the midst of heavy traffic.*
She became frightened and did not know what to do.

_____

_____

3. They had no money left for food.
The last of their money had been spent for the rent.

_____

_____

4. *Their reservation had been made months in advance.*
They were annoyed to find that the hotel had no record of it.

_____

_____

5. *The temperature had been falling rapidly in the last few days.*
The growers were afraid they would lose their entire orange crop.

_____

_____

6. *Classes had been canceled because of bad weather.*
The children watched television all day long.

_____

_____

7. He was able to leave on an early train.
His meeting had ended sooner than was expected.

_____

_____

8. *Traffic had been delayed because of an accident.*
   They missed the first half of the play.

   _____

   _____

9. *The children had not had dinner yet.*
   Their mother quickly began to prepare something for them.

   _____

   _____

10. *The lifeboats had been lowered.*
    The passengers got off the sinking ship.

    _____

    _____

8-2
ABSOLUTE CONSTRUCTIONS WITHOUT PARTICIPLES

Being is implied in such absolute constructions. The chief word in the predicate of the absolute may be: a noun (**his book now a** *bestseller*), an adjective (**his book now** *famous*), an adverb (**his long work finally** *over*), a prepositional phrase (**his book now** *on sale* **at all bookstores**).

Change the italicized sentences to absolute constructions. Omit the verbs in the absolutes. Set off the constructions with commas.

EXAMPLE: a. *The once busy factories are now completely idle.*
         Many people left the town to find work elsewhere.
         The once busy factories now completely idle, many people left the town to find work elsewhere.

        b. *Her husband was out of work.*
         She decided to get a job herself.
         Her husband out of work, she decided to get a job herself.

1. *His eyes were wide open in astonishment.*
   The young boy watched his physics teacher magnetize one object after another.

   _____

   _____

2. *The long hot summer was over.*
   They looked forward to some beautiful fall days.

   _____

   _____

3. *The country was in a state of chaos because of the prolonged war.*
   Many homeless children wandered from village to village in search of food.

   _____

   _____

4. *Her youngest son was already a famous doctor.*
   She boasted about him to all her friends.

   _____

   _____

5. *Their rent was in arrears.*
   They were asked to move.

   _____

   _____

6. *The once wealthy man was now a pauper.*
   He lived by himself in a small furnished room.

   _____

   _____

7. *His fortune was the largest in the world.*
   He could buy anything but happiness.

   _____

   _____

8. The tourists saw a small boy approaching them.
   His clothes were almost in rags, his face was pale and emaciated.

   _____

   _____

9. *The patient was not yet out of danger.*
   Her doctor decided to keep her in the hospital for another week.

   _____

   _____

8-3

WITH ABSOLUTE CONSTRUCTIONS

The word *with* (or its negative *without*) may initiate an absolute construction, making the construction technically a prepositional phrase and thereby relating it grammatically to the rest of the sentence. Such **with** absolutes generally have the same kinds of predicates as absolutes without **with**. **With** often suggests some degree of cause or of **having**.

> The ocean looks very beautiful **with the moonlight glimmering on its surface.**

> **With the police on all sides of them and ready to shoot,** the bank robbers finally surrendered.

Change the italicized sentences to **with** absolute constructions. Note which of these absolutes may also be used without **with**. Note also the choices without the participles; some choices are more acceptable than others.

EXAMPLE: a. *All the representatives were still not there.*
The meeting was postponed for several hours.

With all the representatives still not there, the meeting was postponed for several hours.

b. He was re-elected very quickly.
Not a single vote was cast in opposition.

He was re-elected very quickly, without a single vote (being) cast in opposition. (*or* not a single vote being cast in opposition)

1. *The meeting was set for the following day.*
They had little time to prepare for it.

_____

_____

2. *Her heart was torn between her love for her husband and her love for her parents.*
She spent many sleepless nights deciding what she should do.

_____

_____

3. I can't do any work at all.
There is so much noise all around me. (omit *there*)

_____

_____

4. *People come in and out of the store all day long.*
The storekeeper must watch carefully that nothing is stolen.

_____

_____

5. *All his money is tied up in real estate.*
He has little to invest in the stock market.

_____

_____

6. *A date has not been set for the wedding.* (use *without*)
It is impossible for us to make any plans beforehand.

_____

_____

7. *All the children are at home during the holidays.*
She has a great deal of work to do.

_____

_____

8. *The hot sun was burning down on them hour after hour.*
   The lost travelers despaired of ever getting out of the desert alive.

---

9. *All the roads were blocked by the soldiers.*
   No one could get out of the city.

8-4

POSITION OF ABSOLUTE CONSTRUCTIONS

As loose nonrestrictive elements, the absolute constructions may occupy all three adverbial positions. However, certain types of absolutes are more likely to appear in one position rather than in another.

---

1. **Initial position**—*adverbial clause equivalents that express:*
   a. cause

   The table not having been constructed properly, one of the legs became loose. (= adverbial clause—*because the table had not been constructed properly.*)

   b. time

   Dinner (being) ready, the hostess asked her guests to be seated. (= adverbial clause—*after dinner was ready.* Time may also imply cause.)

2. **Mid-position**—*adjective clause equivalents*

   The children, **many of them only infants,** were left with nothing to eat. (= adjective clause—*many of whom were only infants.*)

3. **Final position**—*coordinate clause equivalents. Such absolutes have a special kind of relationship to the first part of the sentence:*
   a. The absolute gives a further explanation of the first sentence.

   She looks almost like her twin sister, **the only difference being that she is a little taller.**

   b. The absolute represents a "partitioning" of some idea mentioned in the first sentence.

   The men work in two shifts, **the first starting at 8 A.M., the second at 4 P.M.**

   c. The absolute gives descriptive details of a broader subject mentioned in the main clause.

   We could see the mountain from our hotel, **its steep slopes bare of vegetation, its snow-capped peak disappearing into the clouds.**

   d. The absolute refers to an event that occurs simultaneously with the event in the main clause.

   For a long time he lay ill in bed, **the days blending into the nights in one mass of oblivion.**

Absolutes functioning as coordinate clause equivalents may contain infinitives rather than participles—**They decided to row all night,** *all the men to take turns.*

Except for some **with** constructions, absolute constructions are usually cut off with commas.

Care must be taken not to separate a final absolute construction from the preceding part of the sentence.

Change the italicized clauses or sentences to absolute constructions. Keep the absolute constructions in the same position as the italicized clauses or phrases.

EXAMPLE: a. *Because all the restaurants were closed when they arrived,* they had to go to bed hungry.
All the restaurants being closed when they arrived, they had to go to bed hungry.

b. A few of the committee members—*among whom was the chairman*—wanted to investigate the matter immediately.
A few of the committee members—among them the chairman—wanted to investigate the matter immediately.
(Dashes set off an absolute construction more strongly than do commas.)

c. The newspaper is divided into sections.
Each is devoted to a special aspect of the news.
The newspaper is divided into sections, each devoted to a special aspect of the news.

1. *Because the required documents did not arrive on time,* they had to postpone the investigation.

_____

_____

2. *After the children had been fed,* their mother put them to bed.

_____

_____

3. The old house—*whose roof was sagging and whose windows were broken*—was finally put up for sale.

_____

_____

4. The dance is done with couples.
Each executes part of an intricate pattern.

_____

_____

5. The members of the jury could not come to a unanimous decision about the guilt of the accused.
The reason was that the evidence against the defendant was inconclusive.

_____

_____

6. *Because the mining operation proved unprofitable,* the company decided to abandon it.

_____

_____

7. The pupils marched out of the school. *The younger ones preceded the older ones.*

_____

_____

8. *After dinner was over,* the guests went into the living room.

_____

_____

9. *Because their first experiment had been remarkably successful,* they felt encouraged to continue with the other experiments.

_____

_____

10. They looked at each other longingly. *Neither of them spoke a word.*

_____

_____

11. *Because his branch library was closed for the day,* he had to go to the main library to do his research.

_____

_____

12. There was complete silence in the room. *Everyone was too shocked to utter a word.*

_____

_____

13. The graduating students left the school.
    Some were to go on to college, some were to seek employment.

_____

_____

8-5

REVIEW OF ABSOLUTE CONSTRUCTIONS

Combine the following sentences so that the italicized sentence in each group becomes an absolute construction. Use the form of absolute construction suggested in the heading for each group. Use commas to set off the absolute constructions. (In a few final **with** constructions, the commas may be omitted.)

With the Verb

1. The football game was called off.
   The recent storm had made the ground too wet to play.

_____

_____

2. *There were no taxis anywhere in sight.*
    We had to walk.

    _____

    _____

3. Our employees work in two shifts.
    The first starts at 8 A.M., the second at 4 P.M.

    _____

    _____

4. *Our ammunition was exhausted and our water supply was cut off.*
    We were forced to surrender.

    _____

    _____

Without the Verb

5. She sat despondently in a corner.
    Her hands were over her eyes.

    _____

    _____

6. *His three children were now college graduates.*
    He felt he could retire from business.

    _____

    _____

7. The people kept running back and forth.
    All of them were in a terrible hurry.

    _____

    _____

8. The candidate for mayor addressed the audience.
    His tone was confident, forceful, cajoling.

    _____

    _____

Preceded by WITH

With the Verb

9. She looked very pretty.
    Her hair was blowing in the wind.

    _____

    _____

10. The ocean looked particularly beautiful.
    The moonlight was glimmering on its surface.

    _____

    _____

Without the Verb

11. The boy came running into the room.
    His face was dirty and his clothes were all torn.

    _____

    _____

12. The man contemplated suicide.
    All his money was gone and his friends were nowhere in sight.

    _____

    _____

9

Abstract Noun Phrases

Abstract noun phrases may perform all noun functions.

Subject of verb	**His rejection of that good offer** surprises me.
Object of verb	I can't understand **his rejection of that good offer.**
Object of preposition: *in prepositional object* *in adverbial phrase*	We talked about **his rejection of that good offer.** By **his rejection of that good offer,** he showed very poor judgment.
Subjective complement *(predicate noun)*	What I can't understand is **his rejection of that good offer.**
Appositive	I can't understand one thing—**his rejection of that good offer.**

9-1
FORM OF ABSTRACT NOUNS

Nouns that are used as the grammatical head of abstract noun phrases are derived either from verbs or predicate adjectives. Such nouns may be unchanged in form (**to answer,** verb; **an answer,** noun), but more often they have special derivational endings.

Add the derivational suffixes **-ment, -(t)ion, -ance, -ence** to the following *verbs* to form abstract nouns. Make whatever changes are necessary.

develop _____   apply _____

expect _____   resemble _____

solve _____   pronounce _____

encourage _____   enjoy _____

decide _____   persuade _____

recognize _____   interfere _____

avoid _____   separate _____

obey _____   compete _____

determine _____   repeat _____

omit _____   resist _____

depend _____   resign _____

judge _____   tempt _____

Add the derivational suffixes **-(i)ty, -ness, -th** to the following *adjectives* to form abstract nouns. Make whatever changes are necessary.

able _____   probable _____

curious _____   lonely _____

happy _____   moral _____

certain _____   poor _____

equal _____   warm _____

holy _____   severe _____

cruel _____   punctual _____

strong _____   pure _____

loyal _____   scarce _____

prompt _____   simple _____

stupid _____   truthful _____

9-2

"SUBJECTS" IN ABSTRACT NOUN PHRASES

"Subjects" in abstract noun phrases are used in the same way as "subjects" in gerund phrases.

He is responsible for ***the management of the office.***
(implied "subject" of management is **he**)

All his friends were astounded at ***Mr. Smith's arrest for fraud.***
("subject" in possessive form—this form must be used for personal pronoun subjects).

The police were immediately notified about ***the disappearance of the money.***
("subject" in **of** phrase form—the abstract noun phrase is introduced by **the** or another determiner)

Replace the word **this** in one sentence with an abstract noun phrase made from the other sentence. Some "subjects" referring to persons may be either in possessive form or **of** phrase form.

EXAMPLE: a. Bombs were exploding on all sides.
This made the inhabitants fear for their lives.

The explosion of bombs on all sides made the inhabitants fear for their lives.

   b. The Senator argued in favor of the bill.
Many people were convinced by *this*.

Many people were convinced by the Senator's argument(s) in favor of the bill.

(*also* the argument(s) of the Senator)

1. He spoke against his opponent.
This was full of insulting epithets.

_____

2. Planes roared overhead.
For a long time we heard nothing but *this*.

_____

3. People possess firearms. (omit *people*)
This is a misdemeanor.

_____

4. He was upset by *this*.
His secretary resigned.

_____

_____

5. Athletes from many countries participated.
This should make these sports events more interesting.

_____

_____

6. The factory workers were complaining about the long hours.
We sympathize with *this*.

_____

_____

7. He was suspicious of anything new.
   This caused him to be very conservative.

_____

_____

8. His parents are concerned about *this*.
   The boy lacks interest in his school work.

_____

_____

9. He is cruel to his subordinates.
   This has finally been discovered by his employer.

_____

_____

10. A traffic policeman has been assigned to that corner because of *this*.
    Many accidents have occurred there.

_____

_____

11. Abraham Lincoln is responsible for *this*.
    He abolished slavery in 1863. (omit *he*)

_____

_____

12. The Army is sending men to investigate *this*.
    Guerrilla fighters are present in the jungle.

_____

_____

13. The museum has been unable to account for *this*.
    Several precious statues have disappeared.

_____

_____

9-3
"OBJECTS" IN ABSTRACT NOUN PHRASES (1)

In an abstract noun phrase, an original direct object often takes **of** phrase form, or less frequently, possessive form.

> The execution ***of the prisoners*** will cause much public disapproval.
> (compare with the gerund phrase—the executing of the prisoners)
> *or* ***The prisoners'*** execution will cause much public disapproval.

The possessive form is more usual with person-denoting "objects," and is obligatory for personal pronoun "objects"—**his murder, their arrest, our education.**

Make an abstract noun phrase out of the words in parentheses. Use an **of** phrase "object" and begin the phrase with **the** or the possessive of a personal pronoun.

EXAMPLE: a. (employ, highly qualified workers) has greatly increased their production.
<u>The employment of highly qualified workers has greatly increased their production.</u>

              b. He hired an investment broker for (manage, his affairs).
<u>He hired an investment broker for the management of his affairs.</u>

1.   Many people have condemned (employ, slave labor).

2.   Many civil disorders resulted from (assassinate, President).

3.   (she, arrange, flowers) was very lovely.

4.   (they, punish, disobedient children) was very severe.

5.   They were arrested for (possess, marijuana).

6.   (separate, Church and State) is a principle recognized by the American Constitution.

7.   Soon after (destroy, old temple), a new one was built in the same place.

8.   Their teacher was explaining (pronounce, vowels, English).

9.   (solve, problem) is to hire more workers.

10.   (apply, hot compresses) will reduce the swelling.

11.   (seize, Bastille) was the beginning of the French Revolution.

12.   They are always complaining about (they lack, money).

"OBJECTS" IN ABSTRACT NOUN PHRASES (2)

Some prepositionless objects of finite verbs require prepositions other than **of** when they follow the abstract noun derived from the verb.

They requested more money.
vs. Their request for more money.

---

for	*after* demand, desire, pity, preference, request, respect, reverence,
to	*after* address, answer, assistance, damage, injury, obedience, resemblance, resistance, solution
on	*after* attack
in	*after* trust, belief

Sometimes either **for** or **of** may precede a "direct object" in an abstract noun phrase—**her love for** or **of her mother; his admiration for** or **of Shakespeare; his hatred for** or **of all women.**

Change the words in parentheses into an abstract noun phrase. Use the correct preposition before the original direct object.

EXAMPLE: a.   (he, prefer, only daughter) is very obvious.
      His preference for his only daughter is very obvious.

      b.   (he, resemble, father) is very striking.
      His resemblance to his father is very striking.

1.   (damage, flooded area) was so great that the government is declaring it a disaster area.

_____

2.   (child, demand, constant attention) is a sign of great insecurity on her part.

_____

3.   The landlord ignored (tenants, request, more heat).

_____

4.   (he, answer, questions) were not entirely satisfactory to the grand jury.

_____

5.   (they, attack, enemy positions) was unsuccessful.

_____

6.   (he, pity, all stray animals) led him to donate money for an animal shelter.

_____

_____

7.   He began to embezzle money from his clients in order to satisfy (he, desire, more and more, luxuries).

_____

_____

8.   (she, admire, that painter) almost borders on idolatry.

_____

9.   Nothing can shake (he, trust, God).

_____

10.   The most important belief in Schweitzer's religion was (respect, all forms of life).

_____

_____

11.   (The President, address, nation) will be broadcast tonight.

_____

_____

9-5
"COMPLEMENTS" OF NOUNS IN ABSTRACT NOUN PHRASES

Prepositional phrases, infinitive phrases or **that** noun clauses that normally follow verbs or adjectives may also follow the nouns derived from such words.

Prepositional phrases	He atoned for his sins *becomes* **his atonement for his sins**
Infinitive phrases	He decided to take a trip *becomes* **his decision to take a trip**
That noun clauses	He suggested that we see a lawyer *becomes* **his suggestion that we see a lawyer**

Form an abstract noun phrase from the words in parentheses. Be sure to use a prepositional phrase, an infinitive phrase, or a **that** clause after the noun in the abstract noun phrase.

EXAMPLE: a.   (Mr. Jones, persists, his work) will one day bring its own reward.

      Mr. Jones' persistence in his work will one day bring its own reward.

b. No one could understand (he, refuse, accept, award).
No one could understand his refusal to accept the award.

c. (he, pretend, he, have, no money) is utterly ridiculous.
His pretense that he has no money is utterly ridiculous.

1. The foreign student was complimented on (he, was, familiar, English language).

_____

2. He has never broken (he, resolve, not, drink, liquor).

_____

3. (Columbus, assume, world, be, round) has been proved correct.

_____

_____

4. He was overjoyed by (his company, decided, transfer, he, South America).

_____

_____

5. (he, aspired, high position) makes him anxious to know the right people.

_____

_____

6. (he, announce, he, will run, for governor) pleased many of his friends.

_____

_____

7. (marriage counselor, attempt, reconcile, couple) produced no results at all.

_____

_____

8. (residents, complained, they, not have, enough, police protection) was referred to the Chief of Police.

_____

_____

9. When (she, long, her husband) became very great, she called him up long distance.

_____

_____

10. (athlete, was, certain, he, always, win) made him very arrogant.

_____

_____

11. I can understand (a stranger, is, amazed, the size of New York City).

_____

_____

12. (they, are, aware, their mistake) will help them to correct it.

_____

_____

13. (the generals, conspired, overthrow, government) was discovered just in time.

_____

_____

9-6
ADJECTIVES-FROM-ADVERBS IN ABSTRACT NOUN PHRASES

-**Ly** adverbs are changed to adjectives in abstract noun phrases. These -ly adverbs appear originally as modifiers of verbs or predicate adjectives.

> They interrupted his speech **continually** _becomes_
> Their **continual** interruption of his speech.
> (compare with the gerund phrase their **continual** interrupting of his speech)
> He is **extremely** selfish _becomes_ his **extreme** selfishness.

Very before a predicate adjective, and **very much** before a verb usually become the adjective **great** before abstract nouns.

> She is **very** generous _becomes_ her **great** generosity.
> He loved his children **very much** _becomes_ his **great** love for his children.

Form an abstract noun phrase from the words in parentheses. Be careful of the change in form from adverbs to adjectives.

EXAMPLE: a. (the accountant, checked, figures, carefully) revealed several discrepancies.
        The accountant's careful check of the figures revealed several discrepancies.

      b. We couldn't help noticing (she, resembled, her sister, very much).
        We couldn't help noticing her great resemblance to her sister.

      c. The doctors are not able to diagnose (he, has been, ill, recently).
        The doctors are not able to diagnose his recent illness.

1. (he, replied, sharply, her question) hurt her very much.

_____

2. In this state, there is (officials, are elected, annually).

_____

3. (he, was, very successful) has made him very arrogant.

_____

4. (patient, recovered, quickly) surprised even the doctors.

_____

5. The customs officials are requiring (baggage, be inspected, more thoroughly).

_____

_____

6. Because of (she, was, very indignant, his remark) she refused to speak to him again.

_____

_____

7. (they, attended, theater, frequently) has been noticed by some of the actors.

_____

_____

8. (child, was, very curious, his new neighbors) led him to ask some impolite questions.

_____

_____

9. (company, arrived, unexpectedly) disconcerted the hostess.

_____

10. The poor widow thanked him for (he, was, extremely, generous).

_____

11. Our visitors praised (our son, behaved, well).

_____

12. (prices, increased, sharply) will lead to (higher wages, will be demanded, inevitably).

_____

_____

9-7
ABSTRACT NOUN PHRASES
AS ALTERNATIVES FOR DEPENDENT CLAUSES

The abstract noun phrase may be the equivalent of a noun clause or an adverbial clause.

noun clause   ***That her husband failed to keep his word*** disturbed her very much.
or ***Her husband's failure to keep his word*** disturbed her very much.

adverbial clause   **After the Allies defeated the Germans in the First World War,** a peace treaty was signed at Versailles.
or **After the Allies' defeat of the Germans in the First World War,** a peace treaty was signed at Versailles.

Since the abstract noun phrase may have either active or passive meaning, this second clause may also take the form of—**After the defeat of the Germans by the Allies in the First World War.**

Change the italicized clauses to abstract noun phrases.

EXAMPLE: a. *After she was divorced from her husband,* she went on a long trip.
After her divorce from her husband, she went on a long trip.

b. I doubt *that the letter is completely accurate.*
I doubt the complete accuracy of the letter.

1. *Before the incandescent lamp was invented by Edison,* gas was used to light the homes and streets.

_____

_____

2. He promised *that the prisoners would be quickly released.*

_____

3. *Although he was frequently absent from school,* the sick boy was able to do all his assignments.

_____

_____

4. *Until they were rescued at sea,* the men took turns in rowing the boat.

_____

_____

5. In 1776 the American colonies proclaimed *that they were independent.*

_____

6. *Since her husband died,* she has become very moody and depressed.

_____

7. The boy was fired *because he was very inefficient.*

_____

8. It was late in the evening before she noticed *that she had lost an earring.*

_____

_____

9. *Although his doctor had warned him,* he still continued to smoke.

_____

10. *Because someone discovered gold in California in 1848,* many people rushed there hoping to get rich quick.

_____

_____

11. *Although the building had been condemned by the health authorities,* people continued to live in it.

_____

_____

12. *Because the defendant refused to answer some of the questions in court,* some people felt that he was guilty.

_____

_____

9-8
REVIEW OF ABSTRACT NOUN PHRASES

In each set of sentences, replace the word **this** with an abstract noun phrase formed from the other italicized sentence.

Abstract Noun Phrases as Subjects

1. *The doctor arrived quickly.*
   This saved the patient's life.

_____

2. *He loved his wife passionately.*
   This caused him to put up with her nagging habits.

_____

3. *John was unexpectedly dismissed by his company.*
   This disappointed him very much.

_____

4. *Ellen was very ambitious to get ahead.*
   This was the subject of much discussion.

_____

Abstract Noun Phrases as Objects of Verbs

5. *The doctor arrived quickly.*
   I appreciated *this*.

_____

6. *He loved his wife passionately.*
   Everyone could understand *this*.

___

7. *John was unexpectedly dismissed by his company.*
   The union committee is investigating *this*.

___

8. *Ellen was very ambitious to get ahead.*
   Her husband discussed *this*.

___

Abstract Noun Phrases as Objects of Prepositions

9. *The doctor arrived quickly.*
   We were grateful for *this*.

___

10. *He loved his wife passionately.*
    We talked about *this*.

___

11. *John was unexpectedly dismissed by his company.*
    We were surprised at *this*.

___

12. *Ellen was very ambitious to get ahead.*
    Her friends worried about *this*.

___

10

Appositive Phrases

An appositive phrase consists of a predicate complement used alone without a subject or a form of the verb **be.** Its "subject" appears in another part of the sentence.

TYPES OF APPOSITIVE PHRASES

From:

A *predicate noun*	She had asked Mr. Wilson, **a prominent lawyer,** to represent her in court.
A *predicate adjective*	The professor, **unaware that many of his students were asleep,** went right on lecturing.
An *adverb (or adverbial expression)*	The gentleman **over there by the door** is our accountant.
A *prepositional phrase*	Mr. Harris, **in a hurry to get home,** took a taxi from the airport.

10-1
CHANGING ADJECTIVE CLAUSES TO APPOSITIVE PHRASES

Adjective clauses containing a form of **be** may be reduced to appositive phrases by retaining only the complement after **be** (noun, adjective, adverb or prepositional phrase).

The young man, ***who is now a lawyer in a large firm,*** has lost much of his old ambition.

becomes The young man, ***now a lawyer in a large firm,*** has lost much of his old ambition.

The person ***who is responsible for the damage*** will have to pay for it.

becomes The person ***responsible for the damage*** will have to pay for it.

This kind of reduction of adjective clauses is similar to the reduction in participial phrases. In the latter, the subject and a form of the auxiliary **be** are omitted from a passive or a progressive verb.

appositive phrase	The guests (who were) **angry at their hosts' rude behavior,** left without saying goodbye.
participial phrase	The guests, (who were) **angered by their hosts' rude behavior,** left without saying goodbye.

Change the italicized adjective clauses to appositive phrases. Use the same punctuation as the adjective clauses have.

EXAMPLE: a. The young child, *who was the only survivor of the plane crash*, was rushed to the hospital at once.
The young child, the only survivor of the plane crash, was rushed to the hospital at once.

b. The convict, *who was free after twenty years*, came out to a world quite different from the one he had left.
The convict, free after twenty years, came out to a world quite different from the one he had left.

1. We want to see the person *who is in charge of the purchasing department*.

_____

2. Jane, *who is their eldest daughter*, is finishing high school this year.

_____

3. The lecturer on data processing is Professor Nelson, *who is an expert in computer technology*.

_____

4. The volcano, *which has been dormant for over a hundred years*, erupted again with great violence.

_____

_____

5. The Browns, *who were back from their long trip*, began to call all their friends.

_____

_____

6. The old man, *who was a famous athlete in his youth*, talks of nothing but his former accomplishments.

_____

_____

7. The young queen, *who was proud of her royal blood*, tried to be worthy of her heritage.

_____

_____

8. Mathematics, *which was once his favorite subject*, no longer interests him.

_____

9. The deer, *which was too frightened to move,* looked at the hunter so piteously that he could not shoot.

_____

_____

10. We will hire anyone *who is willing to work hard.*

_____

11. Rip Van Winkle, *who had been asleep for many years,* did not recognize his surroundings when he awoke.

_____

_____

12. Their mother, *who was just out of the hospital,* could not take care of the house for several weeks.

_____

_____

13. Students should always do their work in a place *that is conducive to study.*

_____

_____

10-2
"COMPLEMENTS"
OF APPOSITIVE NOUNS AND ADJECTIVES

A. "Complements" of Appositive Nouns

Appositive nouns may be followed by the same types of "complements" as predicate nouns.

Adjective clause	New York, a city **which has seven million people,** has always fascinated me.
Participial phrase	New York, a city **housing seven million people,** has always fascinated me.
Prepositional phrase	New York, a city **of seven million people,** has always fascinated me.

Change the words in parentheses to a "complement"—adjective clause, participial phrase, or prepositional phrase—following the italicized noun head of an appositive phrase. (In some phrases there may be a choice of "complements.") Use a comma at the beginning and end of the appositive phrase.

EXAMPLE: a. One of Shakespeare's most powerful works is *King Lear,* a *play* (it, deals, ingratitude, a man's daughters).
One of Shakespeare's most powerful works is *King Lear,* a play which deals with (or dealing with) the ingratitude of a man's daughters.

b. Ten Main Street, the *address* (the envelope) proved to be incorrect.
Ten Main Street, the address on the envelope, proved to be incorrect.

1. The United States, a *country* (its frontiers, once kept expanding, westward) no longer has a western frontier.

   _____

   _____

2. Philadelphia, the *City* (Brotherly Love) is actually no more friendly than any other city.

   _____

   _____

3. Mr. Olson, the *man* (he, sold, her, car) is a very honest dealer.

   _____

   _____

4. Sally, the *girl* (she, sits, next, me, class) is very pretty.

   _____

   _____

5. It is interesting to read the story of Adam and Eve, the first *people* (they, were created, God).

   _____

   _____

6. The best student, the *one* (he, gets, highest grades) will receive a prize.

   _____

   _____

7. My uncle, the only *person* (he, can do, this kind, work) is out of town now.

   _____

   _____

8. The picture, a *reproduction* (one, in, Louvre) looks very attractive over the couch.

   _____

   _____

9. He will always revere the memory of his mother, a saintly *woman* (she, taught, him, love, his fellowmen).

   _____

   _____

B. "Complements"
of Appositive Adjectives

Appositive adjectives may be followed by the same types of "complements" as predicate adjectives.

That clause	The man, **aware that he had made a mistake,** tried to correct it.
Infinitive phrase	The man, **eager to correct his mistake,** said he would send a revised bill.
Prepositional phrase	The man, **aware of his mistake,** tried to correct it.

Change the words in parentheses to a "complement"—**that** clause, infinitive phrase, prepositional phrase—following the italicized adjective head of an appositive phrase. In some phrases there may be a choice of "complements." Use a comma at the beginning and end of the appositive phrase.

EXAMPLE: a. The young girl, *conscious* (boy, was staring, her), felt very uncomfortable.

  The young girl, conscious that the boy was staring at her, felt very uncomfortable.

  b. The elderly couple, *now free* (do, they pleased), decided to enter a retirement home.

  The elderly couple, now free to do as they pleased, decided to enter a retirement home.

  c. The refugees, *finally safe* (their pursuers), knelt down to give thanks to God.

  The refugees, finally safe from their pursuers, knelt down to give thanks to God.

1. Her father, *unsuccessful* (his business venture), decided to give it up.

_____

_____

2. *Positive* (he, was, right road), the driver refused to consult the map any further.

_____

_____

3. The young couple, *delighted* (they, find, home, last), made big plans for the future.

_____

_____

4. The customer, *indignant* (poor service), complained to the manager.

_____

_____

5. *Happy* (he, see, family, once more), he vowed never to take such a long trip again.

_____

_____

6. *Unaware* (dishonesty, his business partner), he felt sure their business was doing well.

_____

_____

7. *Always loyal* (his company), the young executive never complained about the way he had been treated.

_____

_____

8. The victim of the hotel fire, *lucky* (he, be, alive, himself), mourned for those who had perished in the fire.

_____

_____

10-3
POSITION OF APPOSITIVE PHRASES

The most common position for appositive phrases is after the nouns they refer to.

His uncle, **a proud and unbending man,** refused all help that was offered him.

Charles, **eager to get ahead in his career,** worked hard day and night.

Appositive phrases that refer to the subject of the main verb may also occupy the two other adverbial positions that nonrestrictive participial phrases do.

Initial position	**A proud and unbending man,** his uncle refused all help that was offered him.
	Eager to get ahead in his career, Charles worked hard day and night.
	(In this position, the appositive phrase often expresses *cause*, sometimes *concession*.)
Final position (less common)	His uncle refused all help that was offered him, **a proud and unbending man.**
	Charles worked hard day and night, **eager to get ahead in his career.**

Nonrestrictive phrases require commas in whatever position they are used.

A less common alternative for appositive phrases having the meaning of cause is the participial phrase beginning with **being—Being eager to get ahead in his career.**

Change the italicized adjective or adverbial clauses to nonrestrictive appositive phrases. Be careful of the punctuation. Note all acceptable positions for these phrases.

EXAMPLE: a. The child, *who was afraid to be seen crying,* dried her tears quickly.

The child, afraid to be seen crying, dried her tears quickly.

or Afraid to be seen crying, the child dried her tears quickly.

or The child dried her tears quickly, afraid to be seen crying.

    b. *Because he was happy to receive a promotion,* the young man worked very hard.
       Happy to receive a promotion, the young man worked very hard.
       or The young man, happy to receive a promotion, worked very hard.

    c. *Although he was once calm and considerate of others,* he became eccentric and self-centered in his old age.
       Once calm and considerate of others, he became eccentric and self-centered in his old age.

1. The town, *which was once a prosperous seaport,* is now completely deserted.

_____

_____

2. *Because he was seriously ill,* the boy had to be taken to the hospital at once.

_____

_____

3. The Johnsons, *who were curious about their new neighbors,* went to visit them at the first opportunity.

_____

_____

_____

4. *Because they were desperate about the state of their finances,* the company decided to declare bankruptcy.

_____

_____

_____

5. The young man, *who was bored with college,* decided to drop out and go to work.

_____

_____

6. *Although he was generally gruff and blunt in his behavior,* he was known to be very gentle with children.

_____

_____

7. *Because she was by far the best student in the class,* Jane was chosen to take part in a youth forum on television.

_____

_____

_____

8.   The Italian immigrant, *who was homesick for his native land,* saved enough money to go back for a long visit.

   _____

   _____

   _____

9.   *Because he was deathly afraid of airplanes,* he took the train whenever he could.

   _____

10.   *Although he was a tyrant in the office,* at home he was kind and gentle.

   _____

11.   *Although they were once the best of friends,* the two men stopped speaking to each other because of a bitter quarrel.

   _____

   _____

   _____

10-4
REVIEW OF APPOSITIVE PHRASES

Combine the following sentences so that the italicized sentence contains an appositive phrase.

A. Appositive Noun Phrases

1.   *My neighbor's son is a great collector of stamps.*
   He asks me for every foreign stamp that I get.

   _____

   _____

2.   *Uncle Bob is a veteran of World War Two.*
   He hopes he won't have to fight in World War Three.

   _____

   _____

3.   This furnace is provided with a thermostat.
   A thermostat is a device for controlling the temperature.

   _____

   _____

4.   The leaves are falling from the trees.
   This is an indication that winter is not far away.

   _____

   _____

5. My favorite composer is Beethoven.
   He is a genius of great intensity and complexity.

   _____

   _____

6. Next month I leave for Texas.
   This is the state where everything is bigger and better.

   _____

   _____

7. She has brains, looks, and charm.
   These are the qualities which will help further her great ambition.

   _____

   _____

8. He has gone back to San Francisco.
   San Francisco is the town where he was born.

   _____

   _____

9. The people who made the revolution had high hopes.
   These hopes were dashed by subsequent events.

   _____

   _____

10. Freedom of speech is one of our most cherished constitutional guarantees.
    This guarantee has sometimes been disregarded by different groups in this country.

    _____

    _____

B. Appositive Adjective Phrases

1. This is the story of a normal boy.
   He is proud of his family, his friends, his community.

   _____

   _____

2. *Paul was constantly aware of the criticisms made of him.*
   He found it very hard to follow the dictates of his conscience.

   _____

   _____

3. The harbor is now deserted.
   It was once full of the constant hubbub of arriving and departing ships.

   _____

   _____

4. A new generation has grown up since the war.
    It is no more eager to fight than the previous generation.

    _____

    _____

5. The speaker droned on and on.
    He was unaware that many people in the audience were falling asleep.

    _____

    _____

6. Ahead of us appeared the desert.
    It was silent and grand in the early morning sky.

    _____

    _____

7. Joan of Arc was content to become a martyr for the cause of France.
    She was certain that history would vindicate her some day.

    _____

    _____

8. The ship finally arrived in the harbor.
    It was much the worse for wear after its long journey.

    _____

    _____

9. *She is tired and hungry when she comes home from work.*
    She is always in a bad mood until she rests for a while.

    _____

    _____

10. *Children are fond of excitement in any form.*
    They enjoy big fires as well as little circuses.

    _____

    _____

Final Review

Coordinate and Subordinate Sentence Structures

(Review of Chapter 1–Sentences, Chapter 2– Adverbial Clauses, Chapter 5–Participial Phrases, and Chapter 6–Absolute Constructions)

Combine each set of sentences in as many ways as you can. Make whatever changes are necessary (including additions or omissions), but *preserve the logical relationship between the sentences.* Note the choice of positions and which structures seem more appropriate than others. Be careful of the punctuation.

EXAMPLE: a. The boy was sick.
              He didn't go to school.

              The boy was sick; he didn't go to school.
              The boy was sick, so he didn't go to school.
              The boy was sick; therefore (*or* that's why) he didn't go to school.
              Because (*or* since, as) the boy was sick, he didn't go to school.
              Because of (*or* on account of) his sickness, the boy didn't go to school.
              Being sick, the boy didn't go to school.

         b. The boy was sick.
              He went to school anyhow.

              The boy was sick; he went to school anyhow.
              The boy was sick, but he went to school.
              The boy was sick; however (*or* nevertheless), he went to school.
              Although (*or* even though, though) the boy was sick, he went to school.
              In spite of (*or* despite) his sickness, the boy went to school.

1. Mr. X ate too much.
   He got indigestion.

   _____

   _____

   _____

2. They would like to buy a new house.
   They can't afford one right now.

   _____

   _____

   _____

3. They made very careful preparations.
   Then they did the experiment.

   _____

   _____

   _____

4. Stop driving so fast.
   We'll have an accident.

   _____

   _____

   _____

5. Their plot was discovered.
   The conspirators had to flee for their lives.

   _____

   _____

   _____

6. He suffered a heart attack.
   During this time he was playing tennis.

   _____

   _____

   _____

7. He's studying harder now.
   His grades in school are still very poor.

   _____

   _____

   _____

   _____

8. My wife may call the office.
   In this case, tell her I'll be back in an hour.

   _____

   _____

   _____

   _____

9. We can't grant you any more credit.
   First, all your bills must be paid.

   _____

   _____

   _____

   _____

10. Some people require very little sleep.
    Others need at least eight hours sleep.

    _____

    _____

    _____

    _____

11. Frieda was absorbed in a fascinating novel.
    At the same time her dinner was burning on the stove.

    _____

    _____

    _____

    _____

12. The story might be true or it might be a false rumor.[1]
    In any case, he should not have repeated the story.

    _____

    _____

    _____

    _____

[1]This sentence has a positive-negative condition.

13. He was driving to work.
    He saw an accident.

    _____

    _____

    _____

    _____

14. We must conserve food now.
    If we don't, we'll run short later.

    _____

    _____

    _____

    _____

15. The new bookkeeper was careless.
    The accountant spent a lot of time correcting her mistakes.

    _____

    _____

    _____

    _____

16. He will surely be elected.
    He has promised to end the civil war.

    _____

    _____

    _____

    _____

Adverbials

(Review of Chapter 2–Adverbial Clauses, Chapter 5–Participial Phrases, and Chapter 8–Absolute Constructions)

Combine each set of sentences by *changing the first sentence to an adverbial structure.* Use as many types of adverbial structures as are indicated in the number in parentheses after the first sentence. Some words may need to be omitted from the second sentence in each group. (Do not consider synonyms for conjunctions or prepositions as another choice.)

EXAMPLES: a. The day was too cold for the beach. (2)
       The children had to stay home.
      1. Because (*or* since *or* as) the day was too cold for the beach, the children had to stay home.
      2. The day being too cold for the beach, the children had to stay home.

b. I didn't know you were in the hospital. (2)
Otherwise I would have visited you.
 1. If I had known you were in the hospital, I would have visited you.
 2. Had I known you were in the hospital, I would have visited you.

c. He was severely injured. (4)
But he refused to be taken to the hospital.
 1. Although (*or* though *or* even though) he was severely injured, he refused to be taken to the hospital.
 2. Although severely injured, he. . . .
 3. In spite of (*or* despite) being severely injured, he. . . .
 4. In spite of (*or* despite) his severe injuries, he. . . .

1. We must get new tires for the car. (1)
Otherwise we may have an accident on the road.

_____

_____

2. In the city the pace of life is very fast. (1)
But in the country people move at a more leisurely pace.

_____

_____

3. He was poorly prepared. (4)
But he decided to take the examination.

_____

_____

_____

_____

4. You might see him. (2) (use **should** in one choice)
Give him my regards.

_____

_____

_____

_____

5. The company didn't know how young the boy really was. (2)
Otherwise they would not have hired him.

_____

_____

_____

_____

6. He does everything to please her. (4)[2]
   But she is never satisfied.

   _____

   _____

   _____

   _____

7. The ceiling was very high. (3) (use **great** for **very** in one choice)
   They could never get the room warm enough in winter.

   _____

   _____

   _____

8. There might be a tie for first prize. (2)
   In this case, two awards will be given.

   _____

   _____

9. The labor dispute was finally settled. (2)
   The pilots began to fly the planes again.

   _____

   _____

   _____

   _____

10. He was extremely poor. (3)
    However, he was very proud.

    _____

    _____

    _____

    _____

11. It may rain. (2)
    In this event, the picnic will be canceled.

    _____

    _____

    _____

    _____

[2]Three of the choices require **regardless of, no matter,** and a form ending in **-ever.**

12. The train was very crowded. (2)
    He managed to find a seat.

    _____

    _____

    _____

    _____

13. He wanted to make sure his calculations were correct. (2)
    He checked all of them a second time.

    _____

    _____

    _____

    _____

14. You don't realize how she feels. (1)
    Otherwise you would be more sympathetic.

    _____

    _____

15. She was hired as a bookkeeper. (2)
    She also does secretarial work.

    _____

    _____

    _____

    _____

16. Her boss may approve or he may not. (2)
    In any case, she plans to take her vacation in January.

    _____

    _____

    _____

    _____

17. He disregards what anyone says. (2)
    He always does as he pleases.

    _____

    _____

    _____

    _____

18. She finished her housework. (2)
    Then she watched her favorite TV show.

    _____

    _____

    _____

    _____

19. She took an aspirin. (2)
    She felt better.

    _____

    _____

    _____

20. His fortune was one of the largest in the world. (2)
    He could buy anything but happiness.

    _____

    _____

    _____

21. The examination was very difficult. (3)
    Very few students were able to pass.

    _____

    _____

    _____

    _____

    _____

22. Her health was poor. (2)
    She insisted on keeping her job.

    _____

    _____

    _____

    _____

23. Foreign students in the United States must learn English. (start with **just as**) (1)
    American students in a foreign country must learn the language of that country. (start with **so**)

    _____

    _____

    _____

    _____

24. The doctor advised him to stop smoking. (2)
     He kept right on doing it.

     _____

     _____

     _____

     _____

Adjectivals

(Review of Chapter 3–Adjective Clauses, Chapter 5–Participial Phrases, and Chapter 10–Appositive Phrases)

Change the sentences in parentheses into as many adjective structures as you can. Determine which choice seems best. See which structures can be moved to the beginning of the sentence.
　　Be careful of the punctuation. Use commas with an adjective structure that does not identify or limit further the noun that it modifies.

EXAMPLE:　The children (they were sitting in the last row) are not paying attention to their teacher.
　　　　　　choices:　　who (or that) are sitting in the last row
　　　　　　　　　　　　sitting in the last row
　　　　　　　　　　　　in the last row

1. The meeting (it was held yesterday) was a very important one.

    _____

    _____

    _____

2. Their next-door neighbor (he was arrested for drunken driving) claims he was quite sober.

    _____

    _____

    _____

3. The revolution (it is now in its second year) has caused the complete disruption of the country.

    _____

    _____

    _____

4. Most of the cake (it was to be used for the party) was ordered from the bakery.

    _____

    _____

    _____

5. His youngest brother (he was once a famous football star), now works as an attendant in a gasoline station.

_____

_____

_____

6. The monument (you are looking at it now) is in honor of those men (they were killed in the last war).

_____

_____

_____

7. The money (it was collected for the poor) will be deposited in the bank.

_____

_____

_____

8. It is very quiet in the neighborhood (he lives in this neighborhood).

_____

_____

_____

9. The only thing (you can do this thing now) is to tell the truth.

_____

_____

_____

10. Her eldest son (he is now a popular rock singer) visits her on Mother's Day whenever he can.

_____

_____

_____

11. The flowers (they are grown in this hothouse) are used only for the ruler's palace.

_____

_____

_____

12. They were looking forward to the visit of their relatives (many of the visitors were coming from a considerable distance.)

_____

_____

_____

13.   Children (they are fond of excitement in any form) enjoy big fires as well as circuses.

_____

_____

_____

14.   Her father (he was unsuccessful in his business venture) decided to give it up.

_____

_____

_____

15.   The students in her class (all of them had failed the final examination) had to take it over again.

_____

_____

_____

16.   Mr. Fiorelli (he was homesick for his native land) saved enough money to go back to Italy for a visit.

_____

_____

_____

17.   In the fall the foliage (it is found in New England) is very famous for its brilliant colors.

_____

_____

_____

18.   The passengers (they were tired from the long bus ride) were grateful for the short rest stop the bus made.

_____

_____

_____

19.   The train (it is leaving for Chicago) is ready to receive passengers now.

_____

_____

_____

20.   Columbus (he had discovered America) returned to Spain to tell the queen about the new land.

_____

_____

_____

Nominals (Noun Structures)

(Review of Chapter 4–Noun Clauses, Chapter 6–Gerund Phrases, Chapter 7–Infinitive Phrases, Chapter 9–Abstract Noun Phrases)

A. Four types of grammatical structures may be used in noun function.

1.	*noun clauses*	I urge *that you stay in bed until your fever goes down*.
2.	*gerund phrases*	He admitted *having stolen (or stealing) the car*.
3.	*infinitive phrases*	The guard commanded *the man to halt* at once.
4.	*abstract noun phrases*	*Your assistance in this matter* will be appreciated.

Some nominal structures may be used interchangeably.

I urge you *to stay in bed until your fever goes down*.

He admitted *that he had stolen (or stealing) the car*.

The guard commanded *that the man halt at once*.

Your assisting me in this matter will be appreciated.

Combine the sentences so that the word **this** is replaced by a noun structure formed from the other sentence. Note which structures are more desirable.

EXAMPLE: He violated the law.
This was surprising.

That he violated the law was surprising.
It was surprising that he violated the law.
For him to violate the law was surprising.
His violating the law was surprising.
His violation of the law was surprising.

1. *This* was quite unexpected.
They broke off all negotiations.

_____

_____

_____

2. I can't understand *this*.
They rejected the advice of their lawyer.

_____

_____

_____

3. The city dismissed all the striking firemen.
    This seems unfair.

    _____

    _____

    _____

4. All American pupils learn about *this*.
    The Pilgrims landed at Plymouth Rock in 1620.

    _____

    _____

    _____

5. We must find out *this*.
    Where should we deliver these packages?

    _____

    _____

    _____

6. I can't imagine *this*.
    He would do something wrong. (change *something* to *anything*)

    _____

    _____

    _____

7. *This* was a great tragedy.
    They lost their only son.

    _____

    _____

    _____

8. They are thinking about *this*.
    Should they buy a new car?

    _____

    _____

    _____

9. I anticipated *this*.
    I would have some trouble with them.

    _____

    _____

    _____

10. He denied *this*.
    He acted improperly in the matter.

    _____

    _____

    _____

11. Her husband rejected that good offer.
    This doesn't make sense to her.

    _____

    _____

    _____

12. I recommend *this*.
    Study the report carefully.

    _____

    _____

    _____

13. The hotel was closed unexpectedly.
    This left the tourists with no place to stay.

    _____

    _____

    _____

14. He asked *this*.
    Did anyone call?

    _____

    _____

    _____

15. These figures are being checked carefully.
    This will take a long time.

    _____

    _____

    _____

16. He didn't pay his taxes.
    He was fined for *this*.

    _____

    _____

    _____

17. We overlook our faults.
    This is easy to do.

    _____

    _____

    _____

18. You must arrive early.
    This is very important.

    _____

    _____

    _____

19. The students wanted to know *this*.
    "When will we get our grades?"

    _____

    _____

    _____

20. *This* is essential.
    Everyone must come to the meeting on time.

    _____

    _____

    _____

B. Using the information given in parentheses, construct as many acceptable nominal structures as you can.

EXAMPLE: (anyone, be, home, this hour) is very unlikely.

That anyone should be home at this hour

For anyone to be home at this hour } is very unlikely

Anyone's being home at this hour
    (least desirable choice)

It is very unlikely { that anyone should be home at this hour.

for anyone to be at home at this hour.

1. (she, lose, temper) is very unusual.

    _____

    _____

    _____

    _____

2. (anyone, make, such, mistake) seems incredible.

_____

_____

_____

_____

3. The doctor suggested (she, move, a warmer climate).

_____

_____

_____

4. (a person, can survive, without, food and water) is not possible.

_____

_____

_____

5. The broker advised (they, not invest, money, that company).

_____

_____

_____

_____

6. We would prefer (take, vacation, later in the year).

_____

_____

_____

7. (locate, decent place, live) is the most pressing problem for the young couple.

_____

_____

_____

8. The gardener recommended (they, plant, some shade trees).

_____

_____

_____

9.   (they, flagrantly, violate, law) is very foolish.

_____

_____

_____

10.   The girls' parents don't like (their daughters, stay out, late, night).

_____

_____

_____

11.   (change, one's mind) was once considered a woman's privilege.

_____

_____

_____

12.   (obtain, building license) shouldn't be difficult.

_____

_____

_____

13.   (be, overcharged, anything) enrages her.

_____

_____

_____

14.   He was arrested for (destroy, property, his neighbor).

_____

_____

_____

15.   (consume, too much sugar) is not good for the health.

_____

_____

_____

16. The government requires (people who are going overseas, get, passport).

_____

_____

_____

_____

17. Soon after (destroy, their home, by fire), they built another one on the same site.

_____

_____

_____

_____

18. We look forward (see, you, again, soon).

_____

_____

_____

_____

19. Can you tell me (which road, I take, get to the stadium)?

_____

_____

_____

_____

20. The question for us is (how, get, the money).

_____

_____

_____

_____

APPENDIX 1

Practice Tests

Structure Test 1

Add the required words in the blank spaces. Use only *one word* in a blank. Place an *X* in those blanks where no word is necessary.

1. They had the mechanic _____ fix the car.

2. When we arrive _____ the train station, we'll call you.

3. There were so _____ people in the pool that I couldn't swim.

4. If they had time, they _____ go to the movies.

5. I'm sorry I missed you. I wish I _____ known you were coming.

6. They live _____ 250 Fifth Avenue.

7. What _____ bad weather we are having!

8. He has been away from home _____ January 12.

9. There are some cookies left, aren't _____?

10. He likes the movies, and his wife _____ too.

11. We can't imagine _____ could have wanted to hurt the boy.

12. _____ is something wrong with this typewriter.

13. The family _____ already gone to bed when the telephone rang.

14. Their house was _____ painted when a fire broke out.

15. _____ is too noisy here for us to study.

16. If he had been offered the job, he would _____ refused it.

17. You must take advantage of that offer. It would be foolish not _____

18. He _____ been making a lot of money lately.

19. No one answers the phone. The secretary must _____ having her coffee break.

20. All the students' grades will _____ distributed next week.

21. Let's discuss _____ this matter now.

22. I haven't seen her for a few days. She _____ be sick.

23. When they are young, children have to depend _____ their parents.

24. You _____ not have made such sarcastic remarks to him when you saw him yesterday.

25. What _____ expensive furniture they have!

26. The representatives, many of _____ had come from a great distance, were very tired when they arrived.

27. They entered _____ the room very quietly.

28. The building could have been finished if the workers _____ not gone out on strike.

29. We are interested _____ attending a good school.

30. Please explain _____ me why you did that.

31. _____ quickly the train is going!

32. The office you want is _____ the fifth floor.

33. _____ you hurry, you'll be late.

34. The more money he spends now, _____ less he'll have later.

35. The city _____ he lives in is very large.

36. There are many beautiful shops on _____ Fifth Avenue.

37. _____ marries her will be a lucky man.

38. He studied very hard; _____, he didn't pass the test.

39. The authorities were trying to determine what _____ have caused the plane crash.

40. Do we have to study _____ Chapter Two for tomorrow?

41. The world is getting smaller because of _____ airplane.

42. Only once before in his life _____ he make such a terrible mistake.

43. You'd better study hard; _____, you won't pass the test.

44. They had to call _____ the concert because the singer was ill.

45. He asked _____ his girlfriend to marry him.

46. Most _____ American pupils learn how to read and write.

47. Even _____ they are well prepared, nervous students often do poorly on tests.

48. Some people like to have a vacation in the mountains, while _____ prefer to go to the beach.

49. We _____ eat in order to survive.

50. On the six o'clock news, the weatherman said that it _____ rain after midnight.

Structure Test 2

In each group of sentences, *only one sentence is correct.* Put a circle around the letter before the correct sentence.

1. I'm very poor in English.
   a. Can you suggest me a good English book?
   b. Can you suggest a good English book to me?
   c. Can you suggest good English book?

2. We missed the plane because our train was late.
   a. If our train had come on time, we would have caught the plane.
   b. If our train would have come on time, we would have caught the plane.
   c. If our train had come on time, we would catch the plane.

3. She's in the United States now.
   a. She wishes she were back in her own country.
   b. She wishes she had been back in her own country.
   c. She wishes she is in her own country.

4. Where does the President live?
   a. Someone asked where does the President live?
   b. Someone asked where the President live.
   c. Someone asked where the President lived.

5. *Procrastinate* is a hard word.
   a. What procrastinate means?
   b. What does mean procrastinate?
   c. What does procrastinate mean?

6. Did the children eat their breakfast yet?
   a. They have already ate their breakfast.
   b. They have already eaten their breakfast.
   c. They have already been eaten their breakfast.

7. Can you compare Mary's hat and Jane's?
   a. Mary's hat is the same than Jane's.
   b. Mary's hat is same as Jane's.
   c. Mary's hat is the same as Jane's.

8. How many students in the class passed the examination?
   a. The most of students in the class passed the examination.
   b. Most of the students in the class passed the examination.
   c. The most of the students in the class passed the examination.

9. Everyone was very tired.
   a. However, they continued working until the job was finished.
   b. Moreover, they continued working until the job was finished.
   c. Therefore, they continued working until the job was finished.

10. I can't find Cambodia on this map.
    a. Would you mind to show me where it is.
    b. Would you mind show me where it is.
    c. Would you mind showing me where it is.

11. The party was very enjoyable.
    a. I enjoyed meeting so many interesting people.
    b. I enjoyed to meet so many interesting people.
    c. I enjoyed having meet so many interesting people.

12. I love to go to concerts.
    a. But I'm annoyed if people talk during the music is being played.
    b. But I'm annoyed if people talk while the music is being played.
    c. But I'm annoyed if people talk meanwhile the music is being played.

13. Their father is very strict with the children.
    a. He never lets them to stay out late at night.
    b. He never lets them staying out late at night.
    c. He never lets them stay out late at night.

14. The car isn't running smoothly.
    a. I must have it to be fixed.
    b. I must have it fixed.
    c. I must have it fix.

15. Juan came to the United States a few months ago.
    a. He is still not used to eat American food.
    b. He is still not used to eating American food.
    c. He is still not used eating American food.

16. Maria was baking some cookies last night.
    a. After putting the cookies in the oven, she forgot to turn on the light.
    b. After put the cookies in the oven, she forgot to turn on the light.
    c. After to put the cookies in the oven, she forgot to turn on the light.

17. Does John like to work?
    a. John doesn't like to work, and neither does his brother.
    b. John doesn't like to work, and so his brother doesn't.
    c. John doesn't like to work, and neither his brother does.

18. What were you doing last night?
    a. I was reading a book when some friends came to see me.
    b. I read a book when some friends came to see me.
    c. I was read a book when some friends were coming to see me.

19. Have you seen your aunt recently?
    a. I haven't seen her since two years.
    b. I haven't seen her since 1984.
    c. I haven't seen her during 1984.

20. Who hit the boy?
    a. He was hit by one of his friends.
    b. He was hitted by one of his friends.
    c. He was heat by one of his friends.

21. Would you like to be President?
    a. I prefer be right than President.
    b. I had better be right than President.
    c. I would rather be right than President.

22. The door won't open.
    a. I should not have the right key.
    b. I must not have the right key.
    c. I could not have the right key.

23. Can we put our baggage in the luggage compartment of the train?
    a. No, there are too many baggages there already.
    b. No, there is too much baggage there already.
    c. No, there is too many baggage there already.

24. The students took a very difficult test.
    a. The students what failed the test had to take it again.
    b. The students which failed the test had to take it again.
    c. The students who failed the test had to take it again.

25. Where is Panama?
    a. Panama is a small country located in Central America.
    b. Panama is a small country is located in Central America.
    c. Panama is a small country locating in Central America.

26. When will you call me?
    a. I'll telephone you before I leave the office.
    b. I'll telephone you before I will leave the office.
    c. I'll telephone you before to leave the office.

27. Here is a beautiful dress.
    a. Please try on it.
    b. Please to try it on.
    c. Please try it on.

28. What is the President's name?
    a. I don't know what is the President's name.
    b. I don't know what the President's name is.
    c. I don't know what the President's name.

29. She doesn't feel well.
    a. The doctor recommended that she took a vacation.
    b. The doctor recommended that she takes a vacation.
    c. The doctor recommended that she take a vacation.

30. Who discovered America?
    a. America discovered by Columbus.
    b. America was been discovered by Columbus.
    c. America was discovered by Columbus.

31. How long have you been in the United States?
    a. I am in the United States for five years.
    b. I have been in the United States for five years.
    c. I have been in the United States since five years.

32. Is Carlos still taking classes in English?
    a. No, he stopped to study English last year.
    b. No, he stopped studying English last year.
    c. No, he stopped studying English last year.

33. Do you know the man who is giving the lecture?
    a. Yes, I met him two years before.
    b. Yes, I met him before two years.
    c. Yes, I met him two years ago.

34. The weather is very nice now.
    a. Why not go for a walk?
    b. Why not to go for a walk?
    c. Why not going for a walk?

35. You hurt your sister's feelings.
    a. Why you did that?
    b. What for you did that?
    c. What did you do that for?

36. Why are you laughing?
    a. He said me a funny story.
    b. He told me a funny story.
    c. He said a funny story to me.

37. Their children have very bad manners.
    a. I think their parents did not bring up them well.
    b. I think their parents did not grow them up well.
    c. I think their parents did not bring them up well.

38. What experience in your life was very important to you?
    a. One of the experience that I will always remember was my high school graduation.
    b. One of the experiences that I will always remember it was my high school graduation.
    c. One of the experiences that I will always remember was my high school graduation.

39. When will their wedding take place?
    a. They expect to get married in June.
    b. They expect to get marry in June.
    c. They expect to get marriage in June.

40. When is your birthday?
    a. I born on August 10.
    b. I was born on August 10.
    c. I am born on August 10.

41. Why didn't they hold the meeting?
    a. The meeting was canceled because of the chairman's illness.
    b. The meeting was canceled because of the chairman was ill.
    c. The meeting was canceled. Because the chairman was ill.

42. Where does he live?
    a. The house which he lives is near the post office.
    b. The house he lives in is near the post office.
    c. The house where he lives in is near the post office.

43. Who won the prize?
    a. The man that he won the prize is a professor in my school.
    b. The man which won the prize is a professor in my school.
    c. The man who won the prize is a professor in my school.

44. It's getting cold outside.
    a. We'd better go back in the house.
    b. We better go back in the house.
    c. We'd rather go back in the house.

45. Will they still be there when we arrive?
    a. They will leave by the time we arrive.
    b. They will have left by the time we arrive.
    c. They are going to leave by the time we arrive.

46. How is his English?
    a. He speaks very well English.
    b. He is speaking English very well.
    c. He speaks English very well.

47. Who is going to do the job?
    a. They will do it theirselves.
    b. They will do it themself.
    c. They will do it themselves.

48. Would you care for some coffee?
    a. Yes, I like some.
    b. Yes, I would like some.
    c. Yes, I want it.

49. Was the excursion boat very crowded?
    a. There were too many people on the boat.
    b. There was a lot of people on the boat.
    c. There were too much people on the boat.

50. What is he doing now?
    a. He listen to the radio.
    b. He is listening the radio.
    c. He is listening to the radio.

APPENDIX 2

Practice for the TOEFL Test

EXERCISES

1. Correcting Sentence Faults (faulty parallelism, dangling constructions, run-on sentences, sentence fragments)

2. Improving Sentences (1) (shifts in voice, shifts in tense, shifts in pronouns, shifts from indirect to direct speech)

3. Improving Sentences (2) (excessive or illogical coordination, unnecessary complexity of grammatical structure, misplaced or ambiguously placed modifiers, repetition of words that mean the same thing, *is when* or *is where* used for definition)

4. Subject-Verb Agreement

5. Verbs—Auxiliaries (1)

6. Verbs—Tenses (2)

7. Verbals

8. Word Order (1)

9. Word Order (2)

10. Word Forms

11. Prepositions (1)

12. Prepositions (2)

13. Pronouns

14. Comparison

15. Articles—General Rules (1)

16. Articles—*The* in Names (2)

1. Correcting Sentence Faults

1. Avoid faulty parallelism.

    incorrect: **There is a great difference between dining out and to have a snack at home.**

    correct: **There is a great difference between dining out and having a snack at home.**

    (Structures joined by **and, or, but,** *or* sometimes **not, than,** require the same grammatical form.)

2. Avoid dangling constructions.

    incorrect: **After eating dinner, the table was cleared.**

    correct: **After eating dinner, she cleared the table.**

    or   **After they ate dinner, she cleared the table.**

    (An introductory structure that does not have its own "subject" within it depends on the subject of the main clause for its agent.)

3. Avoid run-on sentences.

    incorrect: **John was sick, he didn't come to school.**

    correct: **John was sick. He didn't come to school.**

    or   **John was sick; he didn't come to school.**
             John was sick, so he didn't come to school.
             Because John was sick, he didn't come to school.

    (Sentences that are not joined by the coordinate conjunctions **and, or, nor, but, so, for, yet** require a semicolon or a period between them.)

4. Avoid sentence fragments.

    incorrect: **She looks almost like her twin sister. The only difference being that she is a little taller.**

    correct: **She looks almost like her twin sister, the only difference being that she is a little taller.**

    or   **She looks almost like her twin sister. The only difference is that she is a little taller.**

    (A complex structure must be attached to the rest of the sentence. Do not cut it off with either a period or a semicolon.)

Rewrite the sentences, correcting faulty parallelism, dangling constructions, run-on sentences, or sentence fragments.

1. Wanting to accomplish something and if you actually accomplish it may not be the same thing.

    _____

    _____

2. Meeting her only once, she enchanted him completely.

    _____

    _____

3. He was deeply hurt by her remarks, however he said nothing in reply.

    _____

    _____

4. The men work in two shifts. The first starting at 8:00 A.M, the second at 4 P.M.

    _____

    _____

5. Not only was she very beautiful, but how intelligent she was.

    _____

    _____

6. By obeying all traffic regulations, many accidents can be avoided.

    _____

    _____

7. He needed to finish an important job, therefore he decided not to go to the conference.

    _____

    _____

8. Some newspapers have no advertising at all. Whereas others carry many advertisements.

    _____

    _____

9. It is better to repeat a noun than making an ambiguous statement.

    _____

    _____

10. I need to improve my English. Because I want to enter an American university.

    _____

    _____

11. It's what you do, not saying it, that counts.

    _____

    _____

12. Having been found guilty by the jury, the judge gave the defendant a severe sentence.

    _____

    _____

13. The favorite spectator sport for Americans is football. While Europeans get excited about soccer.

    _____

    _____

14. They looked at each other longingly. Neither of them speaking a word.

    _____

    _____

15. I must get the money on time, otherwise I can't go on my vacation.

_____

_____

16. As a child, my parents took me to the beach every summer.

_____

_____

17. When ready, take the meat out of the oven immediately.

_____

_____

18. I'll introduce you to my friends. I think you'll like them.

_____

_____

19. He has many accomplishments, for example he is a good sportsman and a fine musician.

_____

_____

20. The company is holding a meeting on production rates, new machinery, and how to improve working conditions.

_____

_____

21. While camping in the mountains, the sight of a huge bear terrified them.

_____

_____

22. The automobile safety belt should be used at all times, it takes only a few seconds to buckle up.

_____

_____

23. His sister is going to buy a new car. Because she needs it for her work.

_____

_____

24. The police surrounded the house but made no attempt to enter it. The idea being that eventually the killer would have to come out.

_____

_____

25. The weather was very hot sometimes the temperature would go up as high as 125 degrees.

_____

_____

26. Blowing at 60 miles an hour, the tree was knocked down by the wind.

_____

_____

27. The book tells about the hardships of the Indians and how they resent living on a reservation.

_____

_____

28. Women should be treated equally in every respect. Whether they choose to work or whether they choose to stay at home.

_____

_____

29. Our language does not have a past tense, we only add a word like yesterday to signify the time.

_____

_____

30. I came to the United States for several reasons. Among them to learn English and to continue my studies.

_____

_____

31. Until you visit my country, you will never know how beautiful it is. And how developed it is.

_____

_____

32. Before leaving the house, all the windows must be closed.

_____

_____

33. At the age of three, my parents were already asking me what I wanted to be when I grew up.

_____

_____

34. While walking in the forest, many beautiful birds can be seen.

_____

_____

2. Improving Sentences (1)

1. Avoid a shift (change) in voice (active-passive).

incorrect: **On Monday I bought a plane ticket and Tuesday was spent getting a vaccination and packing.**

correct: **On Monday I bought a plane ticket, and on Tuesday I got a vaccination and I packed.**

2. Avoid a shift in tense.

incorrect: **The author urges us to eat a balanced meal. He said that fruit and vegetables gave us the vitamins we needed.**

correct: **The author urged us. . . .**

3. Avoid a shift in pronouns used in general statements.

incorrect: **You really never know what love is until we experience it ourselves.**

correct: **We really never know what love is until we experience it ourselves.**

4. Avoid a shift from indirect to direct speech.

incorrect: **Their teacher said that the book was very bad, and why would anyone want to read it.**

correct: **Their teacher said that the book was very bad, and wondered why anyone would want to read it.**

Improve the following sentences by correcting the shifts in voice, tense, pronouns, or the shift from indirect to direct speech.

1. We should remember that we never use the passive when you can use the active.

_____

_____

2. We were driving along the highway when some high mountains were seen from a distance.

_____

_____

3. A good education should enable you to understand what is happening around us.

_____

_____

4. My sister asked me to come to her party and would I come early to help her.

_____

_____

5. We drive our cars on crowded highways and congested streets. Exhaust fumes are inhaled every day.

_____

_____

6. Education not only helps a person get a better job but it shows you how to live a more interesting and fuller life.

_____

_____

7. Some of our students study very hard during the week, but on the weekend, discothèques are frequently visited.

_____

_____

8. In college we often don't have many possibilities to study what you want to.

_____

_____

9. The pharmacist asked what I wanted for my cold, and why had I waited so long to get relief.

_____

_____

10. Freud stresses the fact that the mind is mostly unconscious, and he insisted that neuroses were caused by repressing conflicts in the unconscious mind.

_____

_____

11. In Spanish we have many word endings. Every time you use a verb in a different tense, you need another ending.

_____

_____

12. The author wrote that there was a severe drought at that time. He says that the drought caused many peasants to leave the land.

_____

_____

13. Ideally, students should study what they like, but preparation for a future career should not be neglected.

_____

_____

14. The novel tells about a poor man who is sent to prison for stealing a loaf of bread. The novel went on to tell how he escaped and what happened to him.

_____

_____

15. She said she didn't need her car on the weekend and would I like to borrow it.

_____

_____

16. Learning is a continuous process throughout our lives, as long as you are willing to learn.

_____

_____

17. I began to study the piano when I was six, and it was continued until I left my country.

_____

_____

18. In the city we can find everything you want very easily.

_____

_____

3. Improving Sentences (2)

1. Avoid excessive or illogical coordination.

   Incorrect: **The title of this book is** *The Scarlet Letter* **and it is a story about a woman who commits adultery.**

   Correct: *The Scarlet Letter* **is a story about a woman who commits adultery.**

2. Avoid unnecessary complexity of grammatical structure.

   Incorrect: **If you sail a boat, it's fun.**

   Correct: **Sailing a boat is fun.**

   Incorrect: **In this book, it tells about the great improvement in computers.**

   Correct: **This book tells about the great improvement in computers.**

3. Avoid misplaced or ambiguously placed modifiers.

   Incorrect: **The passengers were told in the morning the ship would sail.**

   Correct: **The passengers were told the ship would sail in the morning.**

   or **In the morning the passengers were told the ship would sail.**

4. Avoid repetition of words that mean the same thing.

   Incorrect: **The people should be given choices in choosing a representative.**

   Correct: **The people should be given a choice of representatives.**

5. Avoid an **is where** or **is when** form of definition.

   Incorrect: **Socialism is where there is no private property.**

   Correct: **Socialism is a system in which there is no private property.**

Improve the following sentences for sentence structure or meaning.

1. At the end, the author finishes this essay by saying he has nothing to gain from his proposal.

_____

_____

2. By serving as a nurse's aide, it gives her something to do in the afternoon.

_____

_____

3. The capital of Korea is located in the northwestern part of Korea and its name is Seoul.

_____

_____

4. Capitalism is where the means of production and distribution are operated privately for profit.

_____

_____

5. A well-known sociologist said recently young people were becoming more serious.

_____

_____

6. I believe that television can be beneficial or harmful depending on the viewer who is watching it.

_____

_____

7. According to the author, he says that women today still do not have full equality with men.

_____

_____

8. In order to qualify for this position, it requires much experience.

_____

_____

9. Van Gogh was a great painter and he once cut off his ear in an irrational moment.

_____

_____

10. In today's newspaper, it has a long article about drug abuse.

_____

_____

11. Although this procedure seems very simple, but it is a basic model for medical students.

_____

_____

12. A sonnet is when a poem has fourteen lines.

_____

13. A man who lies frequently will cheat also.

_____

14. If we are to succeed in our plans, it will require a lot of work.

_____

_____

15.   The book is called *A Farewell to Arms* and it uses the word arms in two senses, and these are the arms of a loved one and the arms used as weapons of war.

_____

_____

16.   The old man was mugged by a youth walking his dog one night.

_____

_____

17.   The most essential and important task in society is to rear children and to form their personalities.

_____

_____

18.   The principal suspended those students who had led the protest because of the school regulations.

_____

_____

19.   For the previous reasons I have already given, this situation can be improved.

_____

_____

20.   In my opinion, I believe that there are several solutions to this problem.

_____

_____

21.   I don't like it when I'm sitting in the subway and an older person comes in and stands near me and constantly looks at me expecting my seat and when I give up my seat he doesn't say anything, because he considers he has the right to it.

_____

_____

22.   Some older people, like for example, those living on a fixed income, are seriously affected by inflation.

_____

_____

4. Subject-Verb Agreement

The form of the verb is singular or plural according to the subject. There are different forms for agreement of the verb only in the present tense, where -s in added for the third person singular verb.

She loves her mother.
vs They love their mother.

Irregular third person singular verbs also end in *-s:* **is, was, has, does.**
The following are specific rules about subject-verb agreement.

1. The verb agrees with the main word in the subject.

   The **material** used for these dresses **is** the best that money can buy.

   However, if the main word of the subject expresses a *part* (*some, all, most, half,* etc.), the verb agrees with the noun in a following *of* phrase.

   Most of the **machinery has** already arrived.
   Most of the **machines have** already arrived.

2. If **each** or **every** is used with the subject, a singular verb must be used.

   Everybody in the class has to write a term paper.

3. Two nouns joined by **and** take a plural verb.

   My aunt and my niece are going to Disneyland.

   However, if a preposition like **together with**, or **as well as** is used instead of **and**, a singular verb is required in formal usage.

   The plant supervisor, as well as the workers, wants greater safety measures to be taken.

4. A noncountable noun requires a singular verb.

   The information in this book is very interesting.

   Examples of noncountable words are **coffee, gold, mathematics, advice, furniture, equipment, scenery, vocabulary, slang, knowledge, news.**

5. In sentences with introductory **there** or **here**, the real subject determines whether the verb is singular or plural.

   There *is a picture* on the wall.
   vs There *are some pictures* on the wall.

6. A subject whose main word is an **-ing** or **- to** form requires a singular verb.

   Writing good letters takes a long time.

7. **A number** (= **some, many**) takes a plural verb.

   A number of students are going home for the holidays.

8. *The number* takes a singular verb.

   The number of students going home for the holidays is small.

Underline the singular or plural verb that is required by the subject.

1. There (is, are) not a lot of television programs suitable for children.

2. Each student (is, are) required to take out health insurance.

3. There (is, are) a long list of jobs to be done before we leave.

4. The information in these reports (is, are) not correct.

5. The news about the patient's recovery (has, have) been very good these days.

6. The star of the show (acts, act) very well, and so (does, do) all the other members of the cast.

7. Their scissors (was, were) not strong enough to cut the wire.

8. The ship's passengers, as well as the entire crew, (was, were) rescued.

9. Here (is, are) the news stories you asked for.

10. The furniture which (was, were) ordered a few months ago (is, are) being delivered now.

11. A program of two very famous films (is, are) being shown tonight.

12. There (has, have) been some signs of improvement in his work.

13. Many a man (has, have) wanted to escape from poverty.

14. The basic knowledge of English and mathematics (has, have) been declining for a decade.

15. The use of symbols in many parts of the story (plays, play) a significant role in bringing out the main theme.

16. There (is, are) a lot of problems that (needs, need) to be discussed.

17. Some of the fruit (was, were) spoiled.

18. A number of the people in this city (lives, live) in poverty.

19. Playing with matches (is, are) very dangerous.

20. Everybody (is, are) coming to see the play.

21. Advertising in that newspaper (costs, cost) a lot of money.

22. To make mistakes (is, are) only human.

23. This year's deficit, together with those of previous years, (has, have) caused the company to go bankrupt.

24. Each of the machines (is, are) carefully inspected before being put into operation.

25. His valuable computer, as well as his important files, (was, were) saved from the fire.

26. On the wall (was, were) several posters.

27. Most of the new equipment (has, have) already been installed in the factory.

28. Equality between men and women (was, were) often not taken for granted in the past.

29. In my country, every house (has, have) a big stone fence.

30. Today's divorce rate is higher than ever because the number of working mothers (is, are) increasing.

5. Verbs—Auxiliaries (1)

1. Use the correct verb form with auxiliaries.

    Examples

BE	+ **-ing** (progressive)	She **is** planting the seeds now. She has **been** planting the seeds all day. She will **be** planting the seeds soon.
BE	+ **-ed** (passive)	The seeds **were** planted last week. The seeds are **being** planted now. The seeds will **be** planted next week. The seeds have already **been** planted.
HAVE	+ **-ed** (perfect)	She **has** already planted the seeds. She will **have** planted the seeds before next week.

    DO   + (no ending) (if there is no auxiliary in the positive statement)

    for questions   **Did** she **plant** the seeds?
    for negatives   She **didn't plant** the seeds.
    for substitution   She planted the same kind of seeds as she **did** last year.

    WILL–WOULD
    SHALL–SHOULD
    CAN–COULD   + (no ending)
    MAY–MIGHT
    MUST

    She **will** (*or* **should, may, must**) **plant** the seeds soon.

2. Use the correct form of irregular verbs with auxiliaries.

    Incorrect: The lesson on verbs was teached yesterday.
    Correct: The lesson on verbs was taught yesterday.
    (For irregular verbs, the second principal part is the past tense; the third principal part is used with the auxiliary **have** for the perfect tenses and with the auxiliary **be** for the passive forms.)

3. Do not omit a required auxiliary with the verb in the predicate.

    Incorrect: While you walking on the street, you can see many magnificent buildings.
    Correct: While you are walking on the street, you . . . .
    (After some conjunctions of time, both the subject and the **be** auxiliary may be omitted—While **walking** on the street, you. . . .)

4. If a verb form refers to compound auxiliaries, make sure this form can apply to **both** auxiliaries.

    Incorrect: We always have, and always will try to serve the public.
    Correct: We have always tried, and always will try to serve the public.

Correct the following sentences containing errors in verb forms.

1. Our club has chose a new president.

_____

2. I needed my uncle's signature on some documents that required by the U.S. Embassy.

_____

_____

3. He doesn't try to help others, and never has.

_____

4. The house has being entirely destroyed by fire.

_____

5. They are discuss that matter now.

_____

6. They watching television when the lights went out.

_____

7. The money that was stole was recovered by the police.

_____

_____

8. They have been meet all day to decide on what course of action to take.

_____

_____

9. There have and always will be some people who believe in dictatorship.

_____

_____

10. When the newlyweds leave the church, rice is throwing at them for good luck and happiness.

_____

_____

11. You should doing your homework instead of watching television.

_____

_____

12. I'm sleepy now because I've ate too much.

_____

13. New York is a city which not reflecting the traditions of the country.

_____

_____

14. The girl has felt on the ice and hurt herself.

_____

15. The repair work in that building already been started.

_____

16. Their teacher would has explained the lesson again if the students had asked her to.

_____

_____

17. Have you ever flew in an airplane before?

_____

18. This monument was build many years ago.

_____

19. That company is more concern about the volume of sales than about the quality of their merchandise.

_____

_____

20. Construction on the bridge was began five years ago.

_____

_____

21. She can and indeed has been competing in every important tennis match in the country.

_____

_____

22. New York is fill with things to do and places to visit.

_____

23. The bank robber has already been catched.

_____

24. She is wear a beautiful suit.

_____

25. He would have win the tennis match if he had not sprained his ankle.

_____

_____

26. He must have been sleep so soundly that he didn't hear the alarm go off.

_____

_____

ɔt like to do the same thing every day.

_____

28. We often serve dinner outdoors, and so does our neighbors.

_____

_____

29. English uses a different writing system than Korean has.

_____

_____

30. I born in Puerto Rico.

_____

31. I moved to the United States after my mother was died.

_____

_____

6. Verbs—Tenses (2)

1. Use the correct tense.

incorrect: In the past, people have traveled by horse and carriage.

correct: In the past, people traveled by horse and carriage.

(Present perfect represents time that comes up to the present. It cannot be used with time that is definitely past.)

incorrect: She writes a letter now.

correct: She is writing a letter now.

(Use the present progressive for present verbs of action.)

2. Use the correct past tense forms of irregular verbs.

incorrect: I seen him yesterday.

correct: I saw him yesterday.

3. Use the correct form after **wish.**

incorrect: They wish they would live in Europe now instead of in the United States.

correct: They wish they lived. . . .

incorrect: I'm catching a cold. I wish I didn't go out in the rain yesterday.

correct: . . . . I wish I hadn't gone out in the rain yesterday.

4. Use the correct verb form for unreal conditional sentences.

incorrect: He would be very happy if he will pass the test.

correct: He would be very happy if he passed the test.

incorrect: He would have passed the test if he studied harder.

correct: He would have passed the test if he had studied harder.

5. Use the correct form in future real conditions or time clauses.

incorrect: When it will stop raining, we'll go for a walk.
correct: When it stops raining, we'll go for a walk.

incorrect: If I will go to the post office, I will get you some stamps.
correct: If I go to the post office, I will get you some stamps.

6. Use the correct tense in sequence of tenses.

incorrect: He asked me how long I have been waiting.
correct: He asked me how long I had been waiting.

(A past main verb usually requires that a following verb, or its auxiliary, also have past form)

7. Use the correct form after verbs of urgency like **suggest, recommend,** or after adjectives of urgency like **important, necessary.**

incorrect: I suggest that you are very careful when you use this machine.
correct: I suggest that you be very careful when you use this machine.

(After verbs or adjectives of urgency, the present subjunctive—the name of the verb, with no change—is used.)

Correct the following sentences containing errors in verb forms.

1. He will not do anything until he will see a lawyer.

_____

_____

2. He pretended that he doesn't understand the question.

_____

_____

3. I wish it would be warmer outside now.

_____

4. If the weather will be good, I'll go to the beach.

_____

5. Up to the twentieth century, many more people in the United States have lived on farms.

_____

_____

6. It is essential that a guard is on duty at all hours of the day.

_____

_____

7. They begun the construction last week.

_____

8.   We recommend that this bill is passed at once.

_____

9.   I wish you told me about this earlier.

_____

10. She prepared dinner when a quarrel broke out among the children.

_____

_____

11. He had many difficulties since he came to this country.

_____

_____

12. After I will wash the dishes, let's have a game of cards.

_____

_____

13. We will take the train if the weather will be very bad.

_____

_____

14. I didn't notice whether she is wearing her wedding ring.

_____

_____

15. Now my office is very busy. I wish I took my vacation when I had the chance.

_____

_____

16. If I felt better yesterday, I would have gone shopping.

_____

_____

17. He requested that all the committee members would be on time.

_____

_____

18. Let's go inside. It begins to rain.

_____

19. I wish I knew you when you were a child.

_____

20. I'm hearing too much static over the radio.

_____

21. If you will see Robert, give him my regards.

_____

22. These days she tries to prepare herself for the medical exam.

_____

_____

23. We just went to bed when the telephone rang.

_____

24. If I knew more French last year, I would have lived in France.

_____

_____

25. It is required that every uniform fits properly.

_____

26. In the past, many marriages have been arranged by matchmakers.

_____

_____

27. Her father teached her how to use the computer.

_____

28. I wish I were with you yesterday.

_____

29. He would help us if he would be here now.

_____

30. It is necessary that everybody takes proper precautions to avoid accidents.

_____

_____

31. She has been writing for many years before one of her novels became a best seller.

_____

_____

32. The company would have been more successful if they had more efficient management.

_____

_____

33.   I was very tired after our hike, so I laid down to rest for a while.

_____

_____

7. Verbals

1. Verbs that follow other verbs should be in the correct form—either in **-ing** form or **to** infinitive form.

incorrect: He stopped to see his friend after a bitter quarrel they had.

correct: He stopped seeing his friend after a bitter quarrel they had.

incorrect: The doctor recommended him to take a long vacation.

correct: The doctor recommended his taking a long vacation.

(The "subject" of the gerund is usually in possessive form—**his.**)

2. Verbs that follow prepositions should be in the **-ing** form.

incorrect: After finish his work, he went to a movie to relax.

correct: After finishing his work, . . .

incorrect: I look forward to see you again.

correct: I look forward to seeing you again.

(**to** after some verbs or adjectives is a preposition rather than the sign of the infinitive.)

3. **To**-less infinitives are used after such auxiliaries as **can, must, would rather, had better.**

incorrect: I would rather to live in the suburbs than right in town.

correct: I would rather live. . . .

4. **To**-less infinitives are used after the verbs **make, have,** *or* **let** (someone **do** something).

incorrect: His mother made him to do his homework before he could watch television.

correct: His mother made him do his homework. . . .

In the following sentences, use the correct form of the verbals.

1.   She always avoids (talk) _____ about this subject.

2.   I can't get used to (type) _____ on this machine.

3.   The bad weather prevented them from (continue) _____ with the construction.

4.   Please excuse me. I must (leave) _____ right away.

5.   Their parents never let the younger children (stay) _____ out after dark.

6.   This method hasn't worked. I suggest your (try) _____ another method.

7.   They have finally finished (paint) _____ their whole house.

8.   Many people have objected to (pay) _____ the increased taxes on their homes.

9. The success of the experiment depends on our (control) _____ the experiment very carefully.

10. You had better not (do) _____ that. You might get into trouble.

11. Doctors often recommend (drink) _____ eight glasses of water a day.

12. The speaker kept on (talk) _____ even after most of the audience had left the hall.

13. I used (pay) _____ all my bills on time, but now I can't.

14. Cover the pan before (put) _____ it in the oven.

15. I had my tailor (make) _____ a woolen suit for me.

16. He is accustomed to (get) _____ up very early in the morning.

17. The thief crept into the house without (be seen) _____ by anyone.

18. I can't afford (buy) _____ a new coat this season.,

19. I enjoyed (see) _____ all the beautiful things in your home.

20. He would rather (work) _____ on a farm than in an office.

21. He deserves (get) _____ a reward for saving the child from the fire.

22. He is opposed to (turn) _____ the building into condominium apartments.

23. It's very hot in here. Would you mind (open) _____ the window.

8. Word Order (1)

1. Do not place an adverbial expression between a verb and its object.

incorrect: I like very much English.
correct: I like English very much.

2. Do not place a pronoun object after a separable (two-part) verb.

incorrect: I don't know this word. I'll look up it in the dictionary.
correct: . . . . I'll look it up in the dictionary.

3. Do not put a *to*-phrase indirect object before the direct object.

incorrect: He gave to his wife some flowers.
correct: He gave some flowers to his wife.
or He gave his wife some flowers.

4. Do not use a long adverbial between the two parts of a verb.

incorrect: The flight attendants were all the time helping the passengers.
correct: The flight attendants were helping the passengers all the time.

5. Use the proper order of adjectives before nouns.

incorrect: an Italian pretty schoolgirl
correct: a pretty Italian schoolgirl

6. Use the proper order of adverbials after verbs.

incorrect: I haven't seen him for a long time at school.
correct: I haven't seen him at school for a long time.
(Adverbials of time are usually placed last.)

7. Place limiting adverbs such as **only, even, hardly, almost** directly before the words they refer to (formal usage).

incorrect: This mistake appears almost on every page. (informal)

correct: This mistake appears on almost every page. (formal)

Correct the mistakes in word order in the following sentences.

1. I make still a lot of mistakes in English.

2. The girl lent to her friend her new typewriter.

3. He sent his office boy at five o'clock to the post office.

4. I will have never again the chance to do this.

5. Several Catholic well-known writers spoke at the conference.

6. I would like to be able to speak more fluently English.

7. The books have finally arrived, so we'll hand out them tomorrow.

8. We will, if we are able to, provide you with whatever you need.

9. Like other countries, we celebrate in Mexico several holidays during the year.

10. The theater may, if not enough tickets are sold, cancel the performance.

11. My country has a river which almost crosses the whole country.

_____

_____

12. The few next years will see many changes.

_____

13. He speaks very well many languages.

_____

14. I've been now five months in this country.

_____

15. Our team didn't even score once.

_____

16. In some news programs they examine more deeply the news.

_____

_____

17. The company sent to their customers a refund.

_____

_____

18. They were planning to have a picnic, but they had to call off it because of the rain.

_____

_____

19. I arrived on December 12 in New York.

_____

20. Some people hardly show any interest in sports.

_____

_____

9. Word Order (2)

1. Use reversed subject-verb order in interrogative-word questions.

incorrect: Why they are going to move?

correct: Why are they going to move?

incorrect: How much cost your umbrella?

correct: How much did your umbrella cost?

(If the verb does not have an auxiliary, a form of the **do** auxiliary is needed unless the question word is the subject—Who bought the umbrella?)

2. Use normal word order in indirect questions (noun clauses).

incorrect: He asked me how much did my umbrella cost.

correct: He asked me how much my umbrella cost.

(Note that the **did** auxiliary is not used in the indirect question.)

If a form of **be** is in the question before a (pro)noun subject (How late **is** the train?), the verb will come after the subject in the indirect question (He asked me how late the train **was.**)

3. Use reversed question order in sentences or clauses beginning with negative adverbials, or with **only,** so.

incorrect: Only with great reluctance he consented to address the audience.

correct: Only with great reluctance did he consent to address the audience.

(Note that the auxiliary **do** is added, as in questions.)

incorrect: He likes the movies, and so his wife does.

correct: He likes the movies, and so does his wife.

Correct the mistakes in word order in the following sentences.

1. Never he had been allowed to do as he pleased.

2. I don't know what is his name.

3. When the store will deliver my purchases?

4. Not only the factory had a burglar alarm system, but it had a watchman night and day.

5. They spend their summers at the beach, and so their neighbors do.

6. Very rarely in my country young couples have their own apartments.

7. I don't know where did they get the money.

8. So rapidly the fire spread that it took many days to get it under control.

_____

_____

9. Why the children don't play outside?

_____

10. Only by hard work a person can succeed.

_____

11. They asked us when did we finish the work.

_____

12. Where you bought that beautiful rug?

_____

13. Under no circumstances you have the right in this country to express your opinions.

_____

14. She doesn't like loud music, and neither her sister does.

_____

_____

15. The author explains to us what were his first impressions of New York.

_____

_____

16. Seldom one can see international or national news on the front page of this newspaper.

_____

_____

17. How long the street will be closed for repairs?

_____

_____

18. The waiter asked them what did they want to order.

_____

_____

19. Who they sold their house to?

_____

20. Not only I began to speak English better, but I began to understand a new culture.

_____

_____

10. Word Forms

1. Use the correct noun ending.
   Identifying nouns:
   by position:
   before a verb (as subject)
   after a verb (as object or subjective complement)
   after a preposition
   by preceding determiners (*the, a, some, my, fourth,* etc.)

incorrect: The reason for my homesick was that I missed my family very much.

correct: The reason for my homesickness was that I missed my family very much.

(The noun **homesickness** appears after the preposition **for** and is preceded by the determiner **my.**)

2. Use the correct adjective ending.
   Identifying adjectives:
   by position:
   before a noun
   after a linking verb (**appear, be, become, get, look, seem,** etc.)
   by preceding words like **very, quite, so**

incorrect: In this country there is freedom for all religion sects.

correct: In this country there is freedom for all religious sects.

(The adjective **religious** appears before the noun **sects.**)

incorrect: My job is not interested at all.

correct: My job is not interesting at all.

(For participial adjectives, the **-ing** ending has *active* meaning—The game was exciting; the exciting game. The **-ed** participle has *passive* meaning—The audience was excited; the excited audience.)

3. Use the correct adverbial ending.
   Identifying adverbs:
   by position:
   initial, mid, final; or before adjectives or other adverbs as modifiers
   by preceding words like **very, quite, so**
   (Many adverbs have **-ly** endings added to adjectives.)

incorrect: The food in this restaurant is incredible good.

correct: The food in this restaurant is incredibly good.

(The adverb **incredibly** appears as a modifier before the adjective **good.**)

4. Use the correct verb ending.
   Identifying verbs:
   by preceding auxiliaries
   or by **to** (for the infinitive)

incorrect: To summary in one sentence, the United States owes much to its colonial heritage.

correct: To summarize in one sentence, the United States owes much to its colonial heritage.

(The verb **summarize** is preceded by **to.**)

In the following sentences, correct the mistakes in word forms.

1. As I got acquaintance with the city, I got to like it more.

_____

_____

2. Can you tell me which points I should emphasis in this report?

_____

_____

3. The number of women who choose not to work after marry has declined.

_____

_____

4. The spirit of equality has broken down all sorts of specially privileges.

_____

_____

5. The men in my country are extremely jealousy about their wives.

_____

_____

6. Very rare are they able to afford to go to the movies.

_____

_____

7. A hurricane caused great destroy in the city.

_____

8. It is unsafety to walk in these streets at night.

_____

9. My language and English have complete different letters.

_____

_____

10. My favorite baseball team has been playing very good lately.

_____

_____

11. He wants to major in electronic.

_____

12. I don't like the house where I'm temporary living.

_____

13. Many television programs have a lot of violent.

_____

14. The news on television is often presented very superficial.

_____

_____

15. He's always very sympathy towards those who appeal to him for money.

_____

_____

16. She is so intelligent that she will success in anything she undertakes.

_____

_____

17. Such an experiment is valid only under rigidly controlling conditions.

_____

_____

18. Venezuela's economic depends on its oil.

_____

_____

19. Spices and herbs act as flavored agents in food.

_____

_____

20. A bomb explosioned yesterday in this building but no one was hurt.

_____

_____

21. San Juan is situated in the north part of Puerto Rico.

_____

_____

22. This machine works more efficient than the old one.

_____

_____

23. The doctor adviced him to get more rest.

_____

_____

24. He made a surprised financial recovery after his bankruptcy.

_____

_____

25. Our government is trying to overcome our political and economical problems.

_____

_____

26. Young children are depend on their parents for love and protection.

_____

_____

11. Prepositions (1)

1. Use the correct preposition after verbs.	*incorrect:* I don't agree to the author's opinion.
	correct: I don't agree with the author's opinion.
2. Use the correct preposition after adjectives.	*incorrect:* Water is composed from hydrogen and oxygen.
	correct: Water is composed of hydrogen and oxygen.
3. Use the correct preposition after nouns.	*incorrect:* His resemblance with his father is very striking.
	correct: His resemblance to his father is very striking.
4. Use the correct preposition to express adverbial meanings (time, place, cause, etc.) or in adverbial expressions.	*incorrect:* Their national convention will take place on March.
	correct: Their national convention will take place in March.
	incorrect: She's going downtown to look at some dresses that are for sale.
	correct: . . . to look at some dresses that are on sale.
5. Use the correct prepositional form in two-part verbs.	*incorrect:* We've just received our new computer. Would you like to try it on?
	correct: . . . . Would you like to try it out?

In the following sentences, supply the correct preposition.

1. Great Britain consists _____ England, Scotland, and Wales.

2. I'm not ashamed _____ anything I've done.

3. All his friends know about his preference _____ beautiful women.

4. He has always behaved _____ a perfect gentleman.

5. The meeting was called _____ because the chairman was ill.

6. After she finished college, she no longer wanted to depend _____ her parents to support her.

7. He's interested _____ buying a diamond ring for his fiancée.

8. His answers _____ our questions were not entirely satisfactory.

9. He is married _____ an ambitious woman.

10. _____ his selfishness, he has very few friends.

11. She likes to go out to dinner very often. Her husband, _____ the other hand, prefers to stay home and watch television.

12. Their bid was turned _____ because it was too high.

13. His reports are always based _____ considerable research.

14. That proposal is not acceptable _____ our company.

15. The office you're looking for is _____ the fifth floor.

16. An urgent matter has come _____ which requires our immediate attention.

17. She has been a teacher _____ five years.

18. I prefer jazz _____ rock music.

19. In accordance _____ your request, we are shipping the books to you immediately.

20. His present behavior is not consistent _____ his behavior in the past.

21. He often turns _____ where he's least expected.

22. When did they arrive _____ the United States?

23. They live _____ 850 Columbia Street.

24. They reproached the child for throwing stones _____ the birds.

25. People who always put _____ doing things until later are called procrastinators.

12. Prepositions (2)

1. Do not use a preposition in front of a subject.

incorrect: By acting as a clown was his way of amusing children.

correct: Acting as a clown was his way of amusing children.

2. If two parallel items cannot be used with the same preposition, each preposition should be included.

incorrect: The long years of drought left many inhabitants without food and complete poverty.

correct: . . . without food and in complete poverty.

3. Do not use a preposition in place of a conjunction.

incorrect: During I'm watching television, the commercials interrupt many times.

correct: While I'm watching television, ...

(The conjunction **while** permits a clause—a subject and a predicate—to follow it.)

or During the time that I'm watching television, ...

(The preposition **during** is followed by a noun object—**time**)

4. Do not omit a required preposition.

incorrect: My uncle waited me at the airport for three hours.

correct: My uncle waited for me. . . .

5. Do not use an unnecessary preposition.

incorrect: He entered into the room so quietly that no one noticed him.

correct: He entered the room so quietly. . . .

incorrect: Most of Japanese are very polite.

correct: Most Japanese are very polite.

In the following sentences, correct the faults in the use of prepositions.

1. I withdrew from the bank enough money to pay this English course.

_____

_____

2. If we don't understand the lesson, we ask to our teacher for help.

_____

3. In New York has more conveniences than Rangoon.

_____

4. The American colonists had a wide experience and knowledge about self-government.

_____

5. This word is very difficult. Please explain me what it means.

_____

_____

6. I have been attending to this class for two months.

_____

7. I remember he mentioned me something about that subject.

_____

_____

8. I'm annoyed when people talk during the concert is going on.

_____

_____

9. Most of American homes have heat and hot water.

_____

10. High school seniors have a great interest and need for gathering information about different colleges.

_____

_____

11. Tomorrow the speaker will discuss about the advantages and the disadvantages of nuclear energy.

_____

_____

12. In spite of they have very little money, they like to dress well.

_____

_____

13. I have been searching the place to start a new life.

_____

14. In my country, which is in the equatorial zone, does not have four seasons.

_____

_____

15. William Shakespeare married to Anne Hathaway in 1582.

_____

_____

16. Because of they are sending their son to an Ivy League college, his wife got a part-time job to help meet the tuition expenses.

_____

_____

17. Despite it was a new experience for me, I felt comfortable in the crowded streets of this new city.

_____

_____

18. Most of high school students ask themselves the question, "Should I go to college?"

_____

_____

19. For those people who do not live in a city will be attracted by the opportunities for entertainment there.

_____

_____

20. He said me, "The post office is two blocks from here."

_____

_____

21. About 7,000,000 of people live in New York City.

_____

22. The city in which I grew up in has changed very much.

_____

_____

23. In Bangkok alone has more than 300 splendid Buddhist temples.

_____

_____

24. Many of young people enjoy dancing at discothèques.

_____

25. Despite of their serious losses in the stock market, they still have plenty to live on.

_____

_____

26. They feel that by going to another country can improve their chances for a better life.

_____

_____

27. I feel that just by sitting in this library will make me concentrate more on my studies.

_____

_____

13. Pronouns

1. Make sure that a pronoun that refers to a preceding noun has the same number (singular or plural) as that noun.

    incorrect: Women once stayed at home to take care of the children, but now she wants to work outside the home.

    correct: . . . but now **they** want to work outside the home.

2. Use the correct subject, object, or possessive form of pronouns.

    incorrect: He received a letter threatening he and his family.

    correct: He received a letter threatening **him** and his family.

    (*Him* is the object of *threatening*.)

3. Use the correct pronoun.

    incorrect: We have seen a change in today's woman, which wants to have a job outside the home.

    correct: . . . today's woman, **who** wants. . . .

    (In an adjective clause, **who** is used for a person, **which** for a thing.) **That** may be used for a person or a thing if there is no comma before it.)

4. Do not use an unnecessary pronoun.

    incorrect: My friend, he told me the whole story.

    correct: My friend told me the whole story.

5. Use the correct form of **other.**

    incorrect: He would like to make friends with many others Americans.

    correct: He would like to make friends with many **other** Americans.

    (**Other** is used with a plural noun; **another** with a singular. (The) **others** is a plural pronoun standing alone—Some people like to vacation at the beach, while **others** prefer the mountains.)

6. Do not omit a pronoun beginning an adjective clause.

    incorrect: My country is located in Southeast Asia is a small one.

    correct: My country, which is located in Southeast Asia, is a small one.

    (The adjective clause can be replaced by a participial phrase—My country, located in Southeast Asia, is a small one.)

7. Use introductory **it** and **there** correctly.

incorrect: It is too much pollution in big cities.
correct: **There** is too much pollution in big cities.
(**There** is used mostly with a *noun* that follows [pollution]. **It** is used with an *adjective* that follows—**It** is **common** to find pollution in big cities. Do not omit introductory **it**.)

In the following sentences, correct the pronoun faults.

1. Anyone which is caught trespassing on this property will be prosecuted.

2. The teacher who he had the greatest influence on me was my English teacher.

3. All the students in the class, because of the long assignment, they asked for more time to do it.

4. It is something wrong with this typewriter.

5. He has always liked to travel to others countries.

6. My country is surrounded by water on three sides, is known for its famous beaches.

7. They invited my wife and I to their silver anniversary party.

8. The student who his books were stolen was quite upset.

9. Every country has it's own social and economic problems.

10. A woman in the ladies auxiliary club didn't like the suggestion. The result was that everyone voted for the plan except she.

_____

_____

11. There are many people of different nationalities live in this city.

_____

_____

12. We appreciated you having helped us last night.

_____

13. My country, which is located in South America and on the Pacific Ocean, it has many mountains.

_____

_____

14. It is a lot of traffic on this street.

_____

15. Is easy for people in this country to buy a car.

_____

16. All what I can do now is to wait for the results of the examination.

_____

_____

17. It is no place like home.

_____

18. This pen doesn't work too well. I'll try the another one.

_____

_____

19. My brother and me are going to the ball game tonight.

_____

_____

20. The people come from other countries like to live in New York.

_____

_____

21. A building which its foundation is not strong may not be able to withstand a hurricane.

_____

_____

22. The subject which I liked it the best in school was English.

_____

_____

23. In Nevada, it is little rainfall and the vegetation is sparse.

_____

_____

24. If teachers have enough time and opportunity, he can shape a student into a better tool for society.

_____

_____

25. They plan to build their new home theirself.

_____

_____

26. A political system that works well in one country may not work so well in other country.

_____

_____

27. There is too noisy for us to study.

_____

28. With who did you go to the party?

_____

29. Some water is not fit to drink it.

_____

30. Inferences may be made without us even realizing it.

_____

_____

31. Who marries her will be a lucky man.

_____

32. A student wants a college education to help them succeed in later life.

_____

_____

33. There's no woman in the world whom he thinks is really good enough for him.

_____

_____

34. A child needs a mother's loving care, especially when they are young.

_____

_____

14. Comparison

1. Use the correct form for the degree of comparison.

   two units: **taller than, more beautiful than**

   three or more units: **the tallest, the most beautiful**

   incorrect: He is the tallest of the two brothers.
   correct: He is the taller of the two brothers.

2. Use the required structure word or word form for comparison.

   the same as
   as . . . as
   different from
   compared with
   in comparison with

   incorrect: My country has the same problems than other developing countries.
   correct: My country has the same problems as other developing countries.

3. Use **like, alike** correctly.

   incorrect: English is alike my language in many ways.
   correct: English is like my language in many ways.
   or English and my language are alike in many ways.

4. Use the required substitute word in comparison.

   one(s), that-those

   incorrect: The salaries we pay for this kind of work are higher than in other companies.
   correct: The salaries we pay for this kind of work are higher than those in other companies.

5. Use **other** where it is logically required in a comparison.

   incorrect: New York City is larger than any city in the United States.
   correct: New York City is larger than any other city in the United States.

6. Avoid ambiguity in making comparisons.

   ambiguous: She likes her teacher better than most of her classmates.
   clearer: She likes her teacher better than most of her classmates do.
   or She likes her teacher better than she does most of her classmates.

In the following sentences, correct the mistakes in comparison.

1. He is the best of the two students who won the prize.

   _____

   _____

2. His grades are about the same than they were last year.

   _____

   _____

3. The life of a worker is often happier than his employer.

   _____

   _____

4. He studies much harder than any student in the class.

_____

_____

5. James appreciates Lucy more than Nancy.

_____

6. My city is quite different with New York.

_____

7. The architecture in my city is more ancient than New York.

_____

_____

8. I think American television programs are worst than the French programs.

_____

_____

9. The prestige of our college is as great as that of any college in this area.

_____

_____

10. Washington is farther from New York than Philadelphia.

_____

_____

11. Comparing with the morning paper, our evening paper has more special features.

_____

_____

12. She is as good a musician as any member of the orchestra.

_____

_____

13. My language, alike English, is written from left to right.

_____

_____

14. Some languages are much more easier to learn than others.

_____

_____

15. The word forms of Spanish are different from that of English.

_____

_____

16. In my country, this is the longest and enjoyable holiday season.

_____

_____

17. La Paz is really a small city comparing with New York.

_____

_____

18. The cultural life of my city differs from it in New York in many respects.

_____

_____

19. The streets in my city are not that safe like they used to be.

_____

_____

20. Many people believe that children respond better to their mother than their father.

_____

_____

21. The streets in New York City are wider than in Kowloon.

_____

_____

22. The two sisters are alike each other in many ways.

_____

_____

23. American television programs are not really very different from the other countries.

_____

_____

24. They think that their country is better than any country in the world.

_____

_____

25. In compare with Great Britain, the United States has very few dialects.

_____

_____

15. Articles
General Rules (1)

---

1. Use an article (**a** or **the**) with a singular countable noun (unless another determiner like **this, their, many, fourth** is used).

incorrect: Author says that the divorce rate has been increasing rapidly.

correct: The author says that the divorce rate has been increasing rapidly.

2. Do not use **the** with a noncountable noun that is not followed by a modifier.

incorrect: The society expects us to conform to its traditional ways.

correct: Society expects us to conform to its traditional ways.

3. Use **the** if a countable or a noncountable noun is narrowed down by a following modifier.

incorrect: Society we live in is becoming more permissive.

correct: The society we live in is becoming more permissive.

incorrect: American corporations are trying to learn from Japanese style of management.

correct: American corporations are trying to learn from the Japanese style of management.

(**Of**-phrase modifiers usually require **the** before the noun, unless another determiner is used.)

4. Use **the** for singular class words in general statements.

incorrect: Computer now has many uses in business and industry.

correct: The computer now has many uses in business and industry.

Also: Computers now have many uses in business and industry.

(The plural form without **the** can also be used as a class word in a general statement.)

5. Use **the** for known or familiar objects:

   in the outside environment

incorrect: Trees are now covered with snow.

correct: The trees are now covered with snow.

But: In northern climates, trees lose their leaves in the winter. **Trees** is a plural class word in a general statement.

   in the inside environment

incorrect: Please put milk over there.

correct: Please put the milk over there.

But: Milk is good for children. **Milk** is a noncountable class word in a general statement.

6. Use **a** with a singular noun having indefinite reference:

   the person or thing is unknown to the speaker

incorrect: Man is here to see you.

correct: A man is here to see you.

the person or thing represents one member of a class

incorrect: Elizabeth is doctor.
correct: Elizabeth is a doctor.
incorrect: Lion is a wild animal.
correct: A lion is a wild animal.
Also: **The** lion. . . . (for the entire class.)

7. Use **the** with superlatives, ordinals, and other "ranking" words (the **first,** the **last,** the **next,** the **following**)

incorrect: Please read second chapter for tomorrow.
correct: Please read the second chapter for tomorrow.
But: Please read Chapter Two for tomorrow. **The** is not used with cardinal numbers.
incorrect: This is last week of registration.
correct: This is the last week of registration.
But: All classes ended last week. **Last** is a point in time.

8. Use **the** in of-phrases after expressions of the quantity (**most of the**)

incorrect: Most of Americans I know have television sets.
correct: Most of the Americans I know have television sets.
or Most Americans I know have television sets.

9. Use **the** with adjectives used as nouns.

incorrect: French celebrate Bastille Day on July 14.
correct: The French celebrate Bastille Day on July 14.

10. Use **such a, what a** with singular countable nouns

incorrect: What beautiful home they have!
correct: What a beautiful home they have!

In the blank spaces, use **a, an,** *or* **the.** If no article is required, place an *X* in the blank space.

1. _____ money is not enough to bring us _____ happiness.

2. Follow _____ street over there until you get to _____ subway.

3. _____ beautiful picture was hanging on _____ wall of _____ bedroom.

4. Please get _____ bread and _____ butter from _____ refrigerator and put them on _____ table.

5. _____ cattle are raised in many parts of this country.

6. _____ doctors recommend _____ aspirin for _____ colds.

7. She is studying _____ Spanish in _____ high school.

8. _____ British and _____ French fought many wars.

9. Kyoto has _____ large population.

10. _____ celebration of our country's independence takes place on July 4.

11. I read _____ story about _____ man living before the American Revolution. _____ man lived at _____ foot of _____ mountains.

12. Because of _____ superstitions, some buildings do not have _____ thirteenth floor.

13. One day I went to _____ friend's house and I noticed something new, _____ beautiful painting.

14. Such _____ small country cannot have _____ diversity of industry.

15. _____ population of Mexico City keeps increasing.

16. _____ automobile has contributed to _____ development of _____ suburbs.

17. He was lying on _____ ground, looking up at _____ moon and _____ stars.

18. This is _____ best book I have ever read.

19. _____ second paragraph gives _____ most important idea of _____ essay we are reading.

20. Most of _____ students in our class passed _____ examination.

21. _____ psychology teaches us a lot about _____ human nature.

22. I began to attend _____ college _____ last year.

23. She is quite _____ good teacher.

24. _____ housework has been made easier because of _____ modern conveniences.

25. In _____ past, it was hoped that _____ younger generation would create _____ new and better society.

26. Many of _____ people whose homes were flooded received _____ financial assistance in order to rebuild their homes.

27. _____ burning of trash outdoors can be dangerous.

28. _____ people I have met so far have been very kind and warm.

29. What _____ beautiful weather we are having!

30. After many months, I finally got _____ visa.

31. In _____ last one hundred years, my city has become

_____ very important center of _____ trade and

_____ culture.

32. _____ Chapter Five is _____ most interesting one

in our textbook.

33. Columbus discovered America in _____ 15th century.

34. _____ history teaches us that _____ same mistakes

can occur again.

16. Articles
THE in Names (2)

Use *The*

1. *geographic names:*
   bodies of water, except lakes and bays—the Mediterranean Sea, the Pacific Ocean, the Nile River—but Lake Erie, Hudson Bay
   names in **of**-phrases—The Gulf of Mexico, the City of New York
   names that end in a word for a political union—The British Commonwealth, the Soviet Union
   plural names—The United States, the Philippines
   Names of general areas using points of the compass (the north, the east, the south, the west)—the Middle East, the South (in the U.S.)—but northern Europe, Southeast Asia (parts of continents)
2. *names of historic events*—The French Revolution, the Renaissance, but World War Two
3. *official titles*—The President, the Prime Minister,—*but* President Lincoln (the name accompanies the title)
4. *names for government bodies*—the Army, the Treasury Department, the police, the highway patrol
5. *names of organizations, institutions*—the United Nations, the Girl Scouts
6. *names of political parties*—the Labor party, the Republican party
7. *names of newspapers*—*The New York Times*, the *Wall Street Journal*
8. *names of museums, libraries, buildings, hotels*—the Metropolitan Museum, the Woolworth Building, the Hilton Hotel

Do *not* use *The*

1. *geographic names*—continents, most countries, states, cities—Africa, Poland, Texas, London
2. names of parks, streets, and avenues—Hyde Park, Fifth Avenue, Broadway
3. names of colleges, universities that do not contain an **of**-phrase in the name—Columbia University—but the University of Pennsylvania
4. *names of holidays*—Thanksgiving Day, Easter—but the Fourth of July
5. *names of most magazines*—*Time Magazine*, *Glamour*

Insert **the** where required. Use an *X* if **the** is not required.

1. _____ United States is bordered on _____ east by _____ Atlantic Ocean and on _____ west by _____ Pacific Ocean.

2. Mark Twain wrote about his experience as a river boat pilot on _____ Mississippi River.

3. _____ Middle Ages is the time in European history between the 5th and the 15th centuries.

4. In the United States, _____ President Washington is revered as the father of our country.

5. _____ American Cancer Society does a lot of research which is designed to help cancer patients.

6. _____ Democratic Party in the United States is known for being more liberal than _____ Republican party.

7. They live near _____ Geneva.

8. _____ Panama Canal is in _____ Central America.

9. They often go to _____ Highland Park to play handball.

10. On _____ Christmas Day, Americans often exchange presents.

11. _____ *Daily News* is a tabloid that concentrates on local news.

12. Karl Marx wrote much of *Das Kapital* in _____ British Museum.

13. _____ World Trade Center consists of two of the tallest buildings in the world.

14. _____ Dominican Republic is in _____ Caribbean Sea.

15. Most of the stores in this town are on _____ Main Street.

16. _____ Princeton University is one of the Ivy League schools.

17. In the United States, many parties are given on _____ New Year's Eve.

18. Another name for _____ Soviet Union is _____ USSR.

19. Right now she's studying at _____ New York University.

20. Trolley cars used to run on _____ 42nd Street.

21. Americans celebrate _____ Independence Day on July 4.

22. _____ prime minister is the chief executive of a parliamentary government.

23. Their son wants to join _____ marines.

24. _____ Scotland is a part of _____ British Isles.

25. Her favorite magazine for news is _____ *Newsweek;* for fashion it is

_____ *Vogue*.

26. _____ *Christian Science Monitor* is considered one of the best newspapers in

the United States.

27. _____ Persian Gulf is rich in oil.

28. _____ Guggenheim Museum in New York was designed by Frank Lloyd

Wright.

29. _____ Industrial Revolution began in England in the late 19th century.

30. _____ Philippines are in _____ Far East.

31. _____ U.S. Armed Forces consist of _____ Army,

_____ Navy, and _____ Air Force.

32. They're staying at _____ Plaza Hotel.

33. To _____ east of _____ India is

_____ Bay of Bengal.

Answers to TOEFL Preparation Section for Part II

ANSWERS TO EXERCISES

(Note: In some sentences, corrections other than the ones given here are also possible.)

1. Correcting Sentence Faults
(pp. 204–207)

1. Wanting to accomplish something and actually accomplishing it . . . .

2. Meeting her only once, he was completely enchanted by her.

3. . . . her remarks; however . . . . (*or* . . . her remarks. However . . . .)

4. The men work in two shifts, the first . . . . (*or* . . . two shifts. The first starts . . . .)

5. Not only was she very beautiful, but she was very intelligent.

6. By obeying all traffic regulations, we can avoid many accidents. (*or* If we obey all traffic regulations, many accidents can be avoided.

7. . . . an important job; therefore . . . . (*or* . . . an important job. Therefore, . . .)

8. . . . at all, whereas others . . . . (*or* . . . at all. Others, however, . . .)

9. It is better to repeat a noun than to make an ambiguous statement.

10. . . . my English because . . . .

11. It's what you do, not what you say, that counts.

12. Having been found guilty by the jury, the defendant was given a severe sentence by the judge. (*or* After the defendant had been found guilty by the jury, the judge gave him . . . .)

13. . . . is football, while Europeans . . . .

14. They looked at each other longingly, neither of them . . . . (*or* . . . longingly. Neither of them spoke a word.)

15. . . . on time; otherwise I can't . . . .

16. As a child, I was taken to the beach by my parents every summer. (*or* When I was a child, my parents took me . . . .)

17. When ready, the meat should be taken out of the oven immediately. (*or* When the meat is ready, take it out . . . .)

18. . . . . my friends; I think you'll . . . . (*or* . . . my friends. I think . . . .)

19. . . . accomplishments; for example . . . .

20. . . . a meeting on production rates, new machinery, and improving working conditions.

21. While camping in the mountains, they were terrified by the sight of a huge bear. (*or* While they were camping in the mountains, the sight . . . .)

22. . . . at all times; it takes . . . . (*or* . . . at all times. It takes . . . .)

23. . . . a new car because she needs it . . . .

24. . . . to enter it, the idea being that . . . . (*or* . . . to enter it. The idea was that . . . .)

25. The weather was very hot; sometimes the temperature . . . . (*or* . . . very hot. Sometimes . . . .)

26. Blowing at 60 miles an hour, the wind knocked down the tree.

27. . . . about the hardships of the Indians and their resentment at living on a reservation.

28. . . . in every respect, whether they choose . . . .

29. . . . a past tense; we only add a word . . . . (*or* . . . a past tense. We only . . . .)

30. . . . several reasons, among them to learn English . . . . (*or* . . . several reasons. Among them were to learn English . . . .)

31. . . . you will never know how beautiful and how developed it is.

32. Before leaving the house, close all the windows. (*or* Before you leave the house, all the windows must be closed.)

33. At the age of three, I was already being asked by my parents what . . . . (*or* When I was three, my parents . . . .)

34. While walking in the forest, you (or we) can see many beautiful birds.

2. Improving Sentences (1)
(pp. 207–210)

1. We should remember that we never use the passive when we can use the active. (*or* use **you** for all three pronouns)

2. We were driving along the highway when we saw some high mountains from a distance.

3. A good education should enable us to understand what is happening around us. (*or* use **you** for both pronouns)

4. My sister asked me to come to her party early to help her.

5. . . . congested streets. We inhale exhaust fumes every day.

6. . . . helps you/us get a better job but it shows you/us how to live . . . . (*or* . . . helps a person . . . but it shows him or her . . .)

7. Some of our students study very hard during the week, but in the weekend, they frequently visit discothèques.

8. In college we often don't have many possibilities to study what we want to. (*Or* use **you** for both pronouns)

9. . . . asked what I wanted for my cold and wondered why I had waited so long . . . .

10. . . . stresses . . . insists . . . . (*or* . . . stressed . . . insisted . . . .)

11. In Spanish we have many word endings. Every time we use a verb in a different tense, we need another ending. (*Or* use *you* for all three pronouns)

12. . . . wrote . . . . said . . . . (*or* . . . writes . . . . says . . . .)

13. Ideally, students should study what they like, but they should not neglect preparation for a future career.

14. . . . tells . . . . goes on . . . (*or* . . . told . . . went on . . . .)

15. She said she didn't need her car on the weekend and asked if/whether I would like to borrow it.

16. . . . throughout our lives, as long as we are willing to learn.

17. I began to study the piano when I was six, and I continued to study until I left my country.

18. In the city we can find everything we want very easily. (*Or* use **you** for both pronouns.)

3. Improving Sentences (2) (pp. 210–212)

1. The author ends by saying he has nothing to gain from his proposal.

2. Serving as a nurse's aid gives her something to do in the afternoon.

3. The capital of Korea, Seoul, is located in the northwestern part of Korea.

4. Capitalism is a system in which the means of production . . . .

5. . . . recently said . . . . (*or* . . . young people recently were . . . .)

6. . . . . or harmful depending on the viewer.

7. The author says that women today . . . .

8. To qualify (*or* qualifying) for this position requires much experience.

9. The great painter Van Gogh once cut off his ear . . . .

10. Today's newspaper has a long article . . . .

11. Although this procedure seems very simple, it is a basic model . . . .

12. A sonnet is a poem of fourteen lines.

13. A man who frequently lies will cheat also. (*Or* A man who lies will frequently cheat also.)

14. To succeed in our plans will require a lot of work.

15. *A Farewell to Arms* uses *arms* in two senses—the arms of a loved one and the arms used as weapons of war.

16. Walking his dog one night, the old man was mugged by a youth.

17. The most essential task in society is . . . .

18. Because of the school regulations, the principal suspended . . . .

19. For the reasons I have given, this situation can be improved.

20. I believe that there are several solutions to this problem.

21. I don't like giving my seat in the subway to an older person who expects it as his right and who doesn't thank me.

22. Some older people living on a fixed income are seriously affected by inflation.

4. Subject-Verb Agreement
(pp. 212–214)

1. are **2.** is **3.** is **4.** is **5.** has **6.** acts, do **7.** were **8.** were **9.** are **10.** was, is **11.** is **12.** have **13.** has **14.** has **15.** plays **16.** are, need **17.** was **18.** live **19.** is **20.** is **21.** costs **22.** is **23.** has **24.** is **25.** was **26.** were **27.** has **28.** was **29.** has **30.** is

5. Verbs
Auxiliaries (1) (pp. 215–218)

1. has chosen **2.** that were required **3.** never has tried **4.** has been entirely destroyed **5.** are discussing **6.** were watching **7.** was stolen **8.** have been meeting **9.** have been and always will be **10.** rice is thrown **11.** should be doing **12.** I've eaten **13.** which does not reflect **14.** has fallen **15.** has already been started **16.** would have explained **17.** Have you ever flown **18.** was built **19.** is more concerned **20.** was begun **21.** She can compete and indeed has been competing **22.** is filled **23.** has already been caught **24.** is wearing **25.** would have won **26.** must have been sleeping **27.** I do not like **28.** so do our neighbors **29.** than Korean does. **30.** I was born **31.** my mother died.

6. Verbs
Tenses (2) (pp. 218–222)

1. until he sees **2.** he didn't understand **3.** it were warmer **4.** If the weather is good **5.** lived **6.** a guard be on duty **7.** began **8.** this bill be passed **9.** you had told me **10.** was preparing **11.** He has had **12.** After I wash **13.** if the weather is **14.** she was wearing **15.** I wish I had taken **16.** If I had felt **17.** the committee members be on time **18.** It is beginning **19.** I wish I had known **20.** I hear **21.** If you see **22.** she is trying **23.** We had just gone to bed **24.** If I had known **25.** every uniform fit properly. **26.** were arranged **27.** taught **28.** I wish I had been **29.** if he were here now **30.** everybody take **31.** She had been writing **32.** if they had had **33.** lay down

7. Verbals (pp. 222–223)

1. talking **2.** typing **3.** continuing **4.** leave **5.** stay **6.** trying **7.** painting **8.** paying **9.** controlling **10.** do **11.** drinking **12.** talking **13.** to pay **14.** putting **15.** make **16.** getting **17.** being seen **18.** to buy **19.** seeing **20.** work **21.** to get **22.** turning **23.** opening

8. Word Order (1) (pp. 223–225)

1. I still make a lot of mistakes in English.

2. The girl lent her new typewriter to her friend.

3. He sent his office boy to the post office at five o'clock.

4. I will never again have . . . . (*or* Never again will I have . . . .)

5. Several well-known Catholic writers . . . .

6. I would like to be able to speak English more fluently.

7. . . . we'll hand them out tomorrow.

8. If we are able to, we will provide you . . . .

9. . . . we celebrate several holidays in Mexico during the year.

10. If not enough tickets are sold, the theater may cancel the performance.

11. . . . which crosses almost the whole country.

12. The next few years . . . .

13. He speaks many languages very well.

14. I've been in this country five months now.

15. Our team didn't score even once.

16. . . . they examine the news more deeply.

17. The company sent a refund to their customers.

18. . . . had to call it off . . . .

19. I arrived in New York on December 12.

20. Some people show hardly any interest in sports.

9. Word Order (2) (pp. 225–227)

1. Never had he been allowed . . . . (*or* He had never been allowed . . . .)

2. I don't know what his name is.

3. When will the store deliver my purchases?

4. Not only did the factory have . . . . (*or* The factory not only had . . . .)

5. . . . and so do their neighbors.

6. Very rarely in my country do young couples have . . . .

7. I don't know where they got the money.

8. So rapidly did the fire spread . . . . (*or* The fire spread so rapidly . . . .)

9. Why don't the children play outside?

10. Only by hard work can a person succeed.

11. They asked us when we finished the work.

12. Where did you buy that beautiful rug?

13. Under no circumstances do you have the right . . . .

14. . . . and neither does her sister.

15. . . . what his first impressions of New York were.

16. Seldom can one see . . . . (*or* One can seldom see . . . .)

17. How long will the street be closed for repairs?

18. The waiter asked them what they wanted to order.

19. Who did they sell their house to?

20. Not only did I begin . . . . (*or* I not only began . . . .)

10. Word Forms (pp. 228–230)

1. As I got acquainted **2.** I should emphasize **3.** after marriage **4.** all sorts of special privileges **5.** are extremely jealous **6.** Very rarely **7.** great destruction **8.** It is unsafe **9.** completely different **10.** very well **11.** electronics **12.** I'm temporarily living **13.** have a lot of violence. **14.** presented very superficially **15.** He's always very sympathetic **16.** she will succeed **17.** under rigidly controlled conditions **18.** Venezuela's economy **19.** as flavoring agents **20.** a bomb exploded **21.** in the northern part **22.** works more efficiently **23.** The doctor advised him **24.** a surprising financial recovery **25.** our political and economic problems **26.** young children are dependent on

11. Prepositions (1) (pp. 231–232)

1. of **2.** of **3.** for **4.** like **5.** off **6.** on, upon **7.** in **8.** to **9.** to **10.** because of **11.** on **12.** down **13.** on, upon **14.** to **15.** on **16.** up **17.** for (may be omitted) **18.** to **19.** with **20.** with **21.** up **22.** in **23.** at **24.** at **25.** off

12. Prepositions (2) (pp. 232–235)

1. . . . to pay for this English course. **2.** . . . we ask our teacher for help. **3.** New York has more conveniences . . . . **4.** . . . a wide experience with (*or* in) and knowledge about self-government. **5.** . . . . Please explain to me what it means. **6.** I have been attending this class for two months. **7.** I remember he mentioned something to me about that subject. **8.** I'm annoyed when people talk while the concert is going on. **9.** Most American homes . . . . **10.** . . . have a great interest in and need for gathering . . . . **11.** . . . will discuss the advantages . . . . **12.** Although they have very little money . . . . **13.** I have been searching for the place . . . . **14.** My country, . . . , does not have four seasons. **15.** married Anne Hathaway **16.** Because they are sending . . . . **17.** Although it was . . . . **18.** Most high school students . . . . **19.** Those people . . . will be attracted by . . . . **20.** He said to me, ... **21.** About 7,000,000 people . . . . **22.** The city in which I grew up has changed very much. (*or* which I grew up in) **23.** Bangkok alone has more than . . . . **24.** Many young people . . . . **25.** Despite their serious losses . . . . **26.** They feel that going to another country can improve their chances . . . . **27.** I feel that just sitting in this library will make me concentrate . . . .

13. Pronouns (pp. 235–238)

1. Anyone who is caught . . . . **2.** The teacher who had . . . . **3.** All the students in the class, because of the long assignment, asked for . . . . **4.** There is something wrong . . . . **5.** . . . to other countries. **6.** My country, which is surrounded . . . . **7.** They invited my wife and me . . . . **8.** The student whose books were stolen . . . . **9.** Every country has its own . . . . **10.** . . . .except her. **11.** There are many people of different nationalities who live in this city. **12.** We appreciated your having helped us last night. **13.** My country, which is located in South America and on the Pacific Ocean, has many mountains. **14.** There is a lot of traffic on this street. **15.** It is easy . . . . **16.** All that I can do now . . . . **17.** There is no place like home. **18.** . . . .I'll try the other one. (*or* I'll try another one.) **19.** My brother and I are going . . . . **20.** The people who come from other countries . . . . **21.** A building whose foundation . . . . **22.** The subject which I liked the best . . . . **23.** In Nevada, there is little rainfall . . . . **24.** If teachers have enough time and opportunity, they can . . . .(*or* If a teacher . . . he or she . . . .) **25.** themselves **26.** . . . in another country. **27.** It is too noisy . . . . **28.** With whom . . . . **29.** Some water is not fit to drink. **30.** . . . without our even realizing it. **31.** Whoever marries her . . . . **32.** A student wants a college education to help him or her . . . .(*or* Students want a college education to help them succeed . . . . **33.** . . . who he thinks is . . . . **34.** A child needs a mother's loving care, especially when he or she is young. (*Or* Children need a mother's loving care, especially when they are young.)

14. Comparison (pp. 239–241)

1. He is the better of the two students . . . . **2.** . . . the same as . . . . **3.** . . . happier than that of his employer. **4.** He studies much harder than any other student in the class. **5.** James appreciates Lucy more than he does Nancy. (*Or* James appreciates Lucy more than Nancy does.) **6.** My city is quite different from New York. (*different than* is informal) **7.** . . . more ancient than that of New York. **8.** . . . are worse than . . . . **9.** . . . as great as that of any other college in this area. **10.** Washington is farther from New York than it is from Philadelphia. (*Or* Washington is farther from New York than Philadelphia is.) **11.** Compared with the morning paper, our evening paper . . . . **12.** She is as good a musician as any other member of the orchestra. **13.** My language, like English, ... **14.** Some languages are much easier . . . . **15.** The word forms of Spanish are different from those of English. **16.** . . . the longest and most enjoyable holiday season. **17.** . . . compared with New York. **18.** . . . differs from that (*or* the one) in New York . . . . **19.** . . . are not as safe as they used to be. **20.** Many people believe that children respond better to their mother than to their father. **21.** . . . are wider than those (*or* the ones) in Kowloon. **22.** The two sisters are like each other . . . .(*or* are alike in many ways) **23.** . . . very different from those (*or* the ones) in other countries. **24.** . . . is better than any other country in the world. **25.** In comparison with Great Britain, . . .

15. Articles
General Rules (1) (pp. 242–245)

1. X, X **2.** the, the **3.** A, the, the **4.** the, the, the, the **5.** X **6.** X, X, X **7.** X, X **8.** The, the **9.** a **10.** The **11.** a, a, The, the, the **12.** X, a/the **13.** a, a **14.** a, a **15.** The **16.** The, the, the **17.** the, the, the **18.** the **19.** The, the, the **20.** the, the **21.** X, X **22.** X, X **23.** a **24.** X, X **25.** the, the, a **26.** the, X **27.** the **28.** The **29.** X **30.** a **31.** the, a, X, X **32.** X, the **33.** the **34.** X, the

16. Articles
The in Names (2) (pp. 245–247)

1. The, the, the, the, the **2.** the **3.** The **4.** X **5.** The **6.** The, the **7.** X **8.** The, X **9.** X **10.** X **11.** The **12.** the **13.** Tne **14.** The, the **15.** X **16.** X **17.** X **18.** the, the **19.** X **20.** X **21.** X **22.** The **23.** the **24.** X, the **25.** X; X **26.** The **27.** The **28.** The **29.** The **30.** The, the **31.** The, the, the, the **32.** the **33.** the, X, the